FISH CULTURE IN YELLOWSTONE NATIONAL PARK

Copyright © 2022 by Frank H. Tainter Ph.D.

ISBN: 978-1-998784-76-9 (Paperback)

   978-1-998784-77-6 (E-book)

All rights reserved. No part of this publication may be reproduced, distributed, or transmitted in any form or by any means, including photocopying, recording, or other electronic or mechanical methods, without the prior written permission of the copyright owner, except in the case brief quotations embodied in critical reviews and other noncommercial uses permitted by copyright law.

The views expressed in this book are solely those of the author and do not necessarily reflect the views of the publisher, and the publisher hereby disclaims any responsibility for them.

BookSide Press
877-741-8091
www.booksidepress.com
orders@booksidepress.com

FISH CULTURE IN YELLOWSTONE NATIONAL PARK

The Early Years: 1900-1930

By

Frank H. Tainter Ph.D.

Fish Lake and hatchery buildings, 1927. Tainter collection.

Contents

Acknowledgements..vii
   The Setting..1
   The Fishes of Yellowstone..6
Spawn Collection and Fish Culture..15
Natural Spawning..22
Artificial Spawning..23
Spawn Collection at Clear Creek...28
Administration -
   Spearfish 40
   Bozeman 51
   Homer..55
Development of The Facilities..68
   Living Conditions at The Lake Hatchery in 1925...........71
Fish Lake and The Soda Butte Station..87
   Remembrances of Fish Lake...90
The Boats..95
The Way There 99
The Rangers..116
Herbert Hoover, Secretary of Commerce...119
Calvin Coolidge, President of The United States 121
The Wonder of It All...125
Bear Me in Mind..137
   Another Bear Story 143
   More Bears...145
Information Sources..148
Notes For The Chapters 157
Artificial Spawning..160

Administration 161
The Boat Drawings 173
Additional Photos 177
Recipe From Fish Car No. 10– Spanish Omelet 187

*Information sign and mess hall, Lake Hatchery, 1927.
Tainter collection.*

ACKNOWLEDGEMENTS

During the early 20th century, as the conservation movement swept across the country, artificial stocking with trout, and other fishes, of fresh-water lakes and streams in the United States reached almost crusade proportions. Although much work was done by individual states, the old U. S. Bureau of Fisheries was responsible for a major portion of this effort. Large quantities of trout spawn were needed. Only one area in the country produced large enough amounts of natural trout spawn to allow such a massive federal effort to be successful-these were the lakes and streams of Yellowstone National Park which contained what is probably the largest inland cutthroat trout population in the world. Between 1889 and 1957, collections of cutthroat trout from the Yellowstone Lake spawn collection operation totaled an estimated 818 million eggs [1].

Following exploratory spawn collection efforts in 1901, certain permanent and seasonal employees of the Bureau of Fisheries were detailed to Yellowstone Park during the summer to collect the naturally produced trout spawn and ship it to other parts of the country for production of fry. Some fry and fingerlings were later also produced in the Park and in the Grand Tetons for stocking of those areas. Because that work was necessarily seasonal, administration of the program was conducted from permanent federal fish hatcheries including those at Spearfish, South Dakota; Bozeman, Montana; and Homer, Minnesota.

The rather remarkable organization of personnel from various states, their equipment, and efficient and successful collection and shipment of trout spawn to all parts of the country has never been adequately documented or considered from a historical viewpoint. Most of the participants in this adventure are deceased and related records have been scattered or lost. Because his uncles, grandfather, and father worked on that program, the author inherited some unique information and photographs of that effort.

In 1986, the University Research Grant Committee of Clemson University provided a small grant of $1,450 to defray expenses to visit two collections of non-circulating archival material pertaining to the spawn collection program. At about this same time, the author contacted an old friend of the family and participant in the Yellowstone fish spawn collection adventure, Roger P. (Bill) Tanner, to see if he would record his recollections of the program. He responded with a great deal of information, much of which is included in this publication.

*Grand Canyon of the Yellowstone River, 1927.
Tainter collection.*

Frank H. Tainter Ph.D.

THE SETTING

Yellowstone Park contains a remarkable assemblage of natural scenic beauty: wildlife, lakes, geysers, and other thermal phenomena. From viewing such wonders as the Mammoth Hot Springs, Undine Falls, the Petrified Forest, Tower Falls, Soda Butte and Fish (now Trout) Lake, Mt. Washburn, the Grand Canyon of the Yellowstone River with the Upper and Lower Falls, the Virginia Cascades, the Golden Gate, Obsidian Cliff, the Norris Geyser Basin, the Midway Geyser Basin, Biscuit Basin, Black Sand Basin, Old Faithful, Kepler Cascades, West Thumb, Yellowstone Lake, the Natural Bridge, Sylvan Pass, LeHardy Rapids, and the Sulphur Caldron, early visitors to the park shortly after it was established as a national park in 1872 were filled with the wonderment and awe of privileged interlopers in a strange and wonderful land.

Along with the wonderment came a sense of disbelief at the productivity of some of Yellowstone's waters. Lake Yellowstone was known as a place where "elegant fish can be forked up by the boat load" [1]. Never before had most visitors seen so many fish, and so easy to catch. But, things were not as perfect in paradise as they seemed. Early explorers found some waters to be abundant with fish, while other areas were barren of fish [2]. In general, the streams in the western half of the Park were barren of fish. Early viewers thought this condition due to the noxious effects of the chemicals and warm water produced by the hot springs [3]. It was some time before it was generally realized that fish were absent because of the obstruction of stream channels by waterfalls.

The fish propagation program in Yellowstone directly owes its beginnings to the attentions of Captain F. A. Boutelle, who in 1889, initiated a program of stocking the barren streams and lakes [4]. Captain

Boutelle, an ardent angler, knew of the barren condition of some lakes and streams and was interested in stocking these. In 1889, he wrote to Colonel Marshall McDonald of the newly formed U. S. Fish Commission of his intent and requested assistance. The fledgling bureaucracy was in need of solidifying its responsibilities so Col. McDonald visited the park and initiated a stocking program. Plants were made in August and September of 1889. David Stan Jordan was to perform a reconnaissance of the condition of all the waters that would provide a basis for future fish-stocking activities [6]. Colonel McDonald, of the newly formed U.S. Fish Commission, welcomed the chance to develop sport fishery in the new park. The 1890s saw a flurry of stocking, primarily of introducing exotic fishes at the expense of native species. Fortunately, many of these attempted stockings, such as smelt in Lake Yellowstone, were not successful [5].

The suggestion in 1889 by Captain J. B. Erwin that a fish hatchery be established was to have far reaching effects that would forever alter one aspect of the natural state of the park. Although today we might not give an ecological blessing for what they did, we must admire them for the purpose and zeal with which they approached the task. Their story is worth recording for it is a unique part of the history of Yellowstone Park.

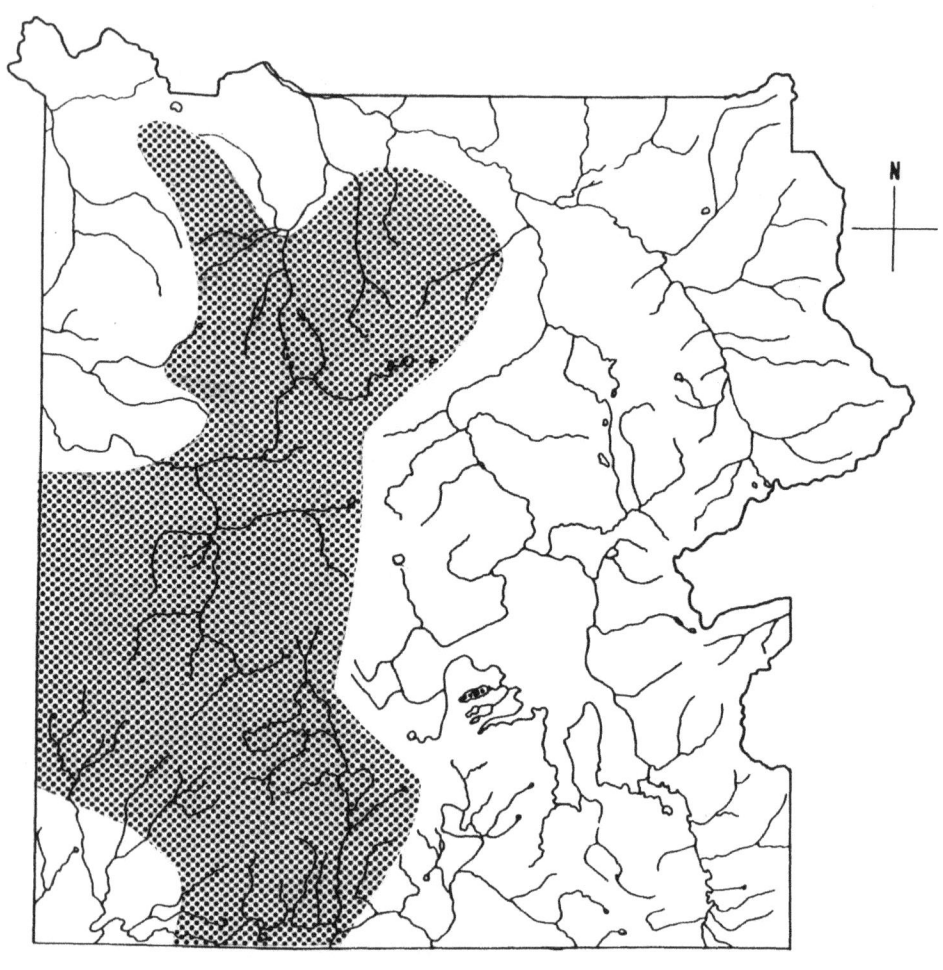

That portion (shaded) of Yellowstone Park that was fishless when European man came [4].

Fish Culture in Yellowstone National Park

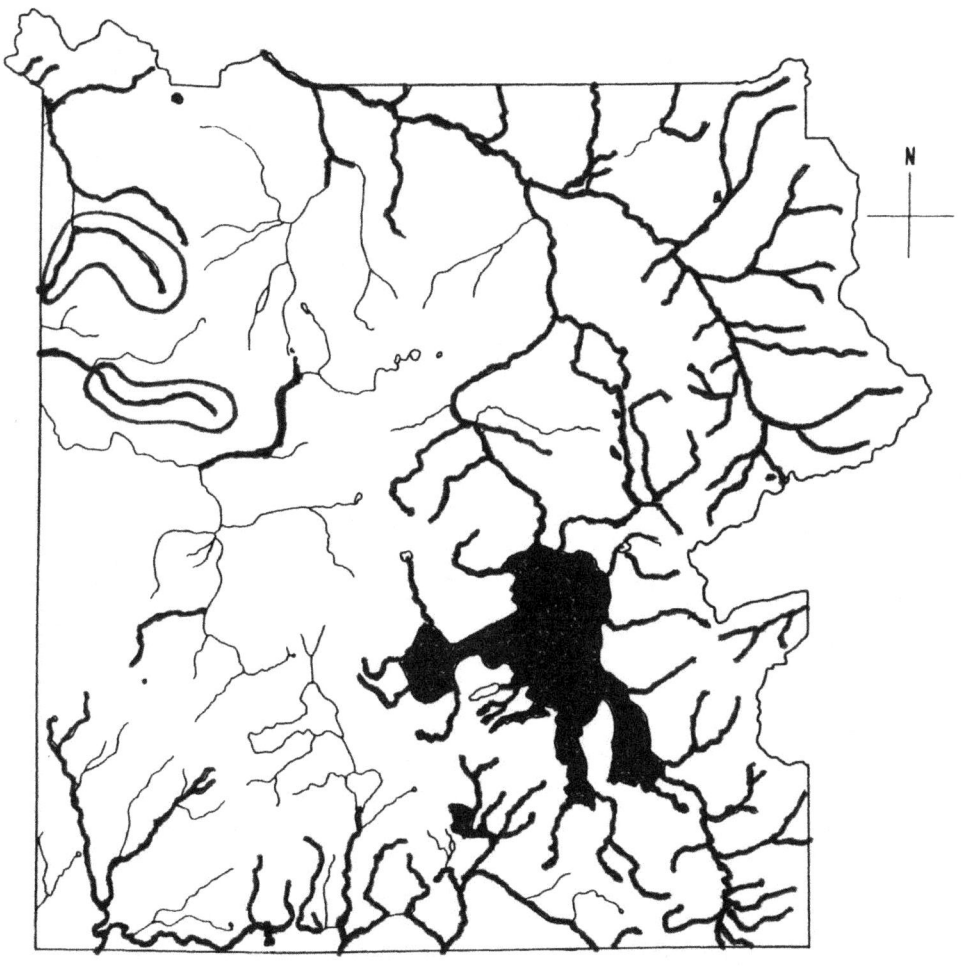

The present distribution of cutthroat (heavy lines) trout and westslope (circled) cutthroat trout in Yellowstone streams.

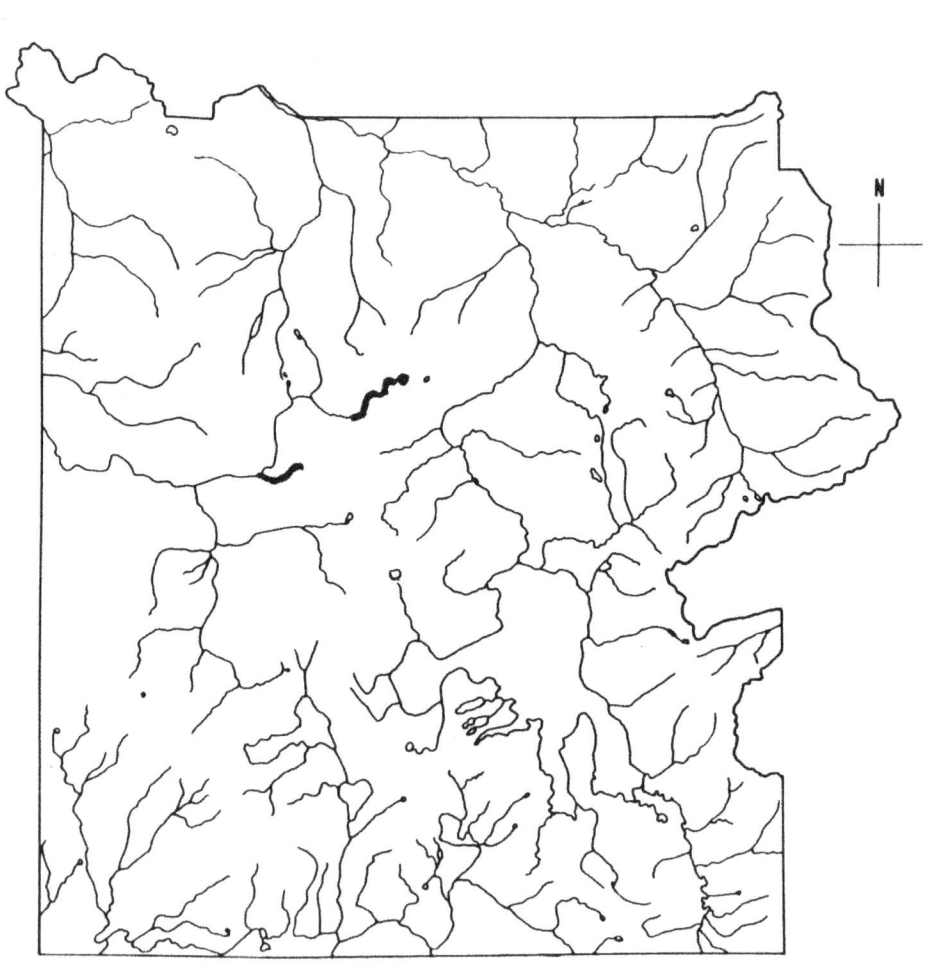

The present distribution (heavy lines) of Montana grayling in Yellowstone streams.

The Fishes of Yellowstone [1]

The major game fish in Yellowstone Park at the present include: Yellowstone cutthroat trout, Montana grayling, rainbow trout, Von Behr and Loch Leven brown trout, eastern brook trout, and lake trout.

The Yellowstone cutthroat trout (known formerly as the black-spotted trout) was native to the Yellowstone River and its tributaries that did not have prohibitively high falls. Early spawn collection programs concentrated on egg collections of this species. During the entire history of that operation, nearly 818 million trout eggs (mostly cutthroat) were collected. Most were transported out of the park for stocking of other waters, although stocking inside the park was done as well. The Firehole drainage was stocked in about 1924.

The Montana grayling was once native to several creeks and rivers within the park but no longer exists in any stream in which it was once native. It is now found in Cascade, Grebe, and Wolf Lakes. The headwaters of the Gibbon River and Grebe Lake were stocked in 1921. An egg collecting station was located at Grebe Lake from 1931-1956 and supplied nearly 72 million eggs that were shipped to at least 14 states. Graylings were stocked in the Madison River in 1934.

Von Behr and Loch Leven brown trout are not native to the North American continent. They were first brought to this country from Europe in 1882 and to Yellowstone Park in 1890. They were stocked in Nez Perce Creek, a major tributary of the Firehole River. They spread and populated other parts of the Madison River drainage, including the Firehole and the Gibbon Rivers. They were stocked in the Madison River in 1929. They are less adaptable to temperature extremes and, thus, move to cooler waters and tributaries. They need good cover and are very difficult to catch and, for this reason, don't need as much protection as do some of the other fish species.

Rainbow trout are native to western North America but were not native to the park. They are extremely adaptable and, thus, were extensively used in fish hatchery stocking. Rainbows were placed in the Gibbon River above Gibbon Falls in about 1889.

Fish Culture in Yellowstone National Park

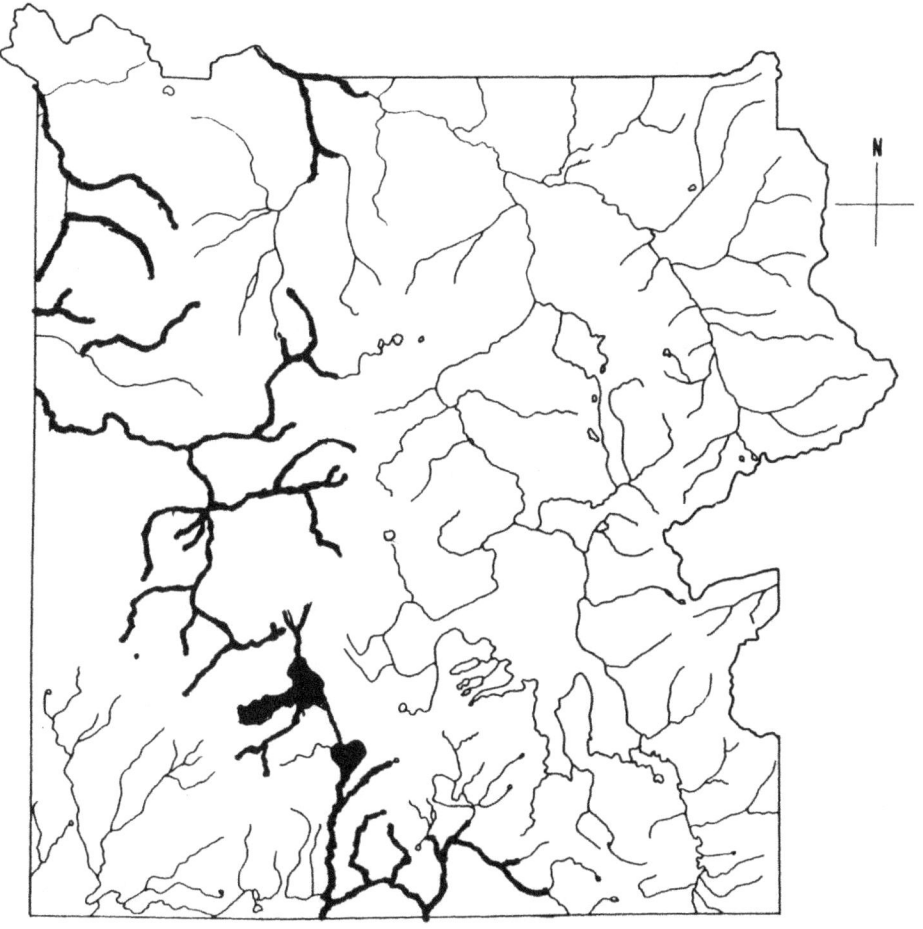

The present distribution (heavy lines) of brown trout in Yellowstone streams and lakes.

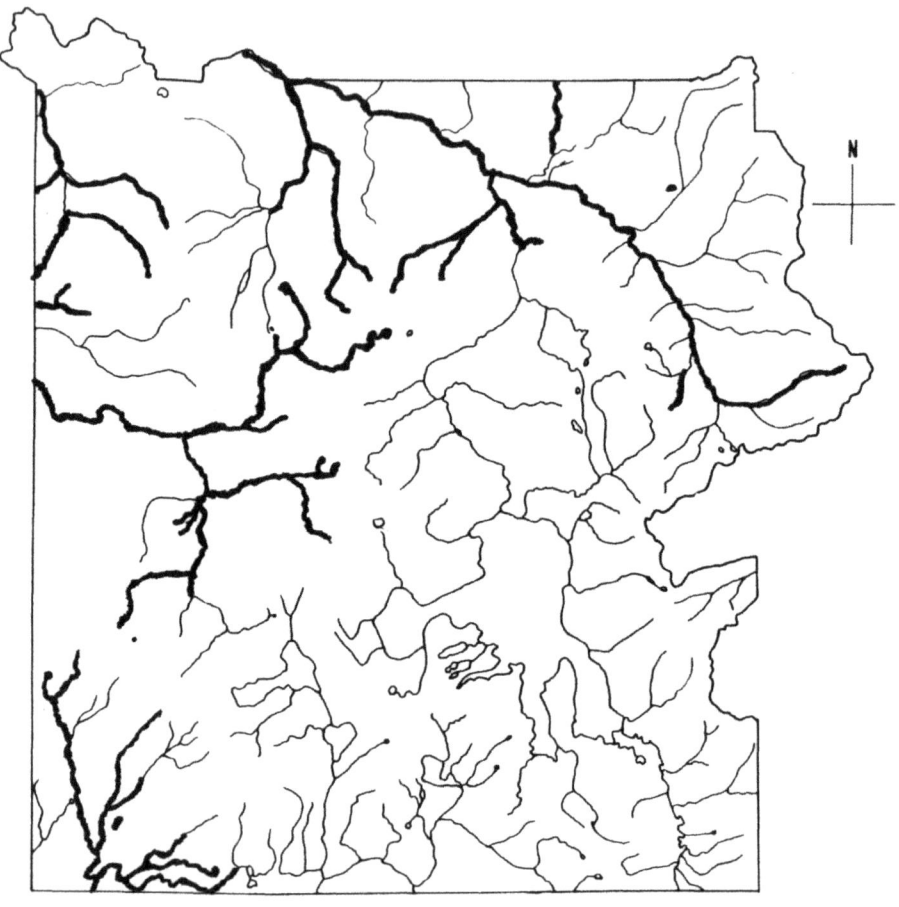

The present distribution (heavy lines) of rainbow trout in Yellowstone streams.

In 1907, D. C. Booth, who was in charge of the Yellowstone spawn collection field operation, planted rainbow trout in Lake Yellowstone. They were first placed in the Firehole drainage in 1922 (Little Firehole River) and 1923 (Nez Perce Creek). They were introduced in the Madison River in 1930. They readily cross with cutthroat trout, but pure populations still exist in some waters.

The eastern brook trout is common in many areas of the park and has done very well in cold, clear headwater lakes and creeks. It tends to overpopulate its habitat and is easily caught. It was first placed in the then-fishless upper Firehole River in 1889.

Lake trout are native to a few lakes in Montana and were introduced to Yellowstone Park in 1890 in the fishless Lewis and Shoshone Lakes and about one century later into Yellowstone Lake. They are now abundant in these lakes and in Heart Lake. In Yellowstone Lake, they have nearly displaced the native cutthroat population. Early commercial fisheries on Lewis and Shoshone Lakes provided fresh lake trout for the park hotels until this practice was stopped in 1917.

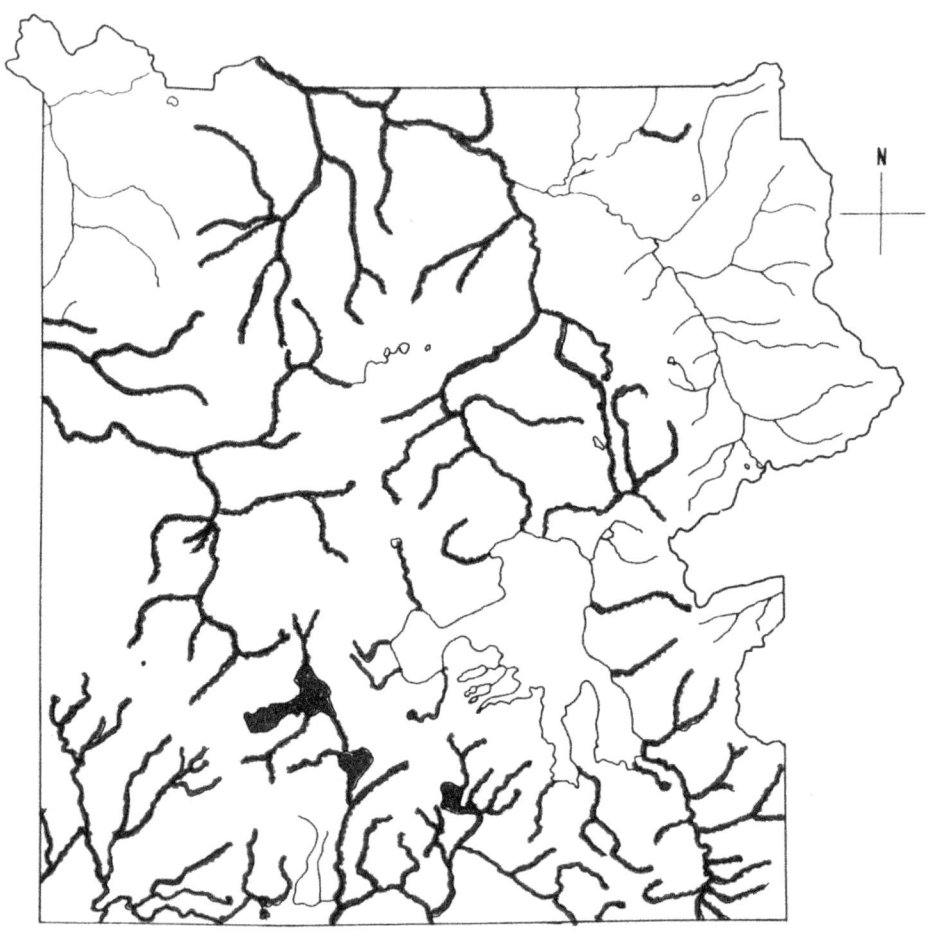

The present distribution (heavy lines) of eastern brook trout in Yellowstone streams and lakes.

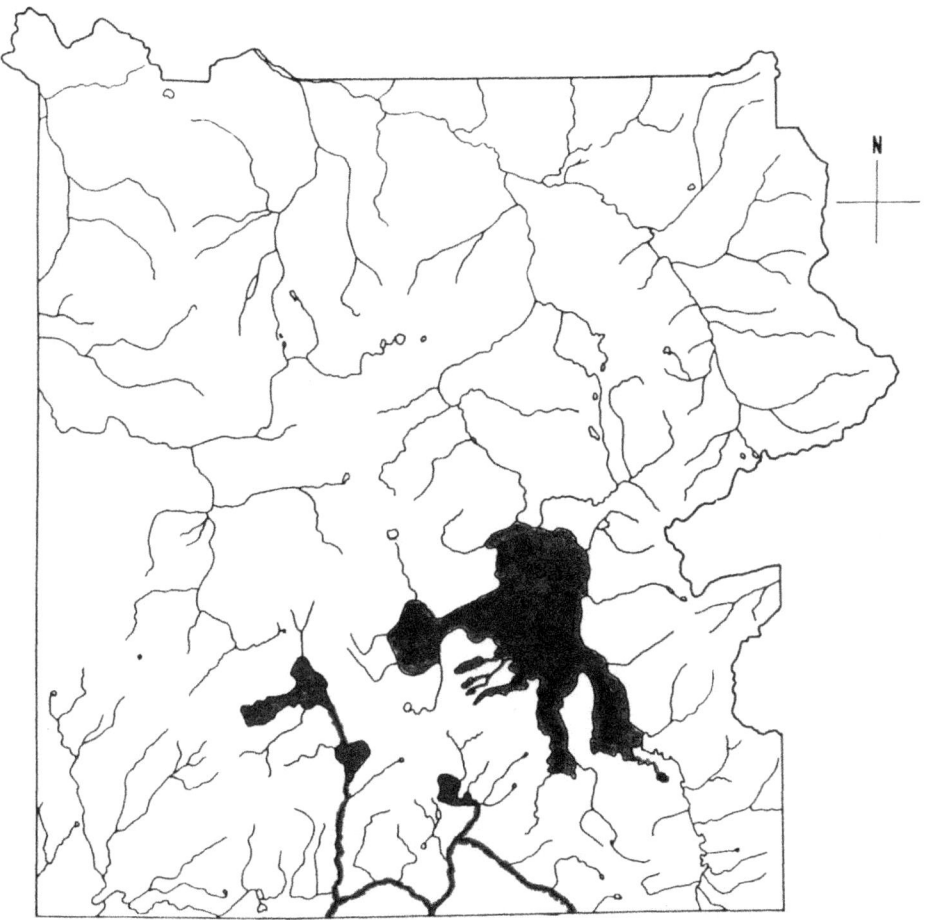

The present distribution (heavy lines) of lake trout in Yellowstone streams and lakes.

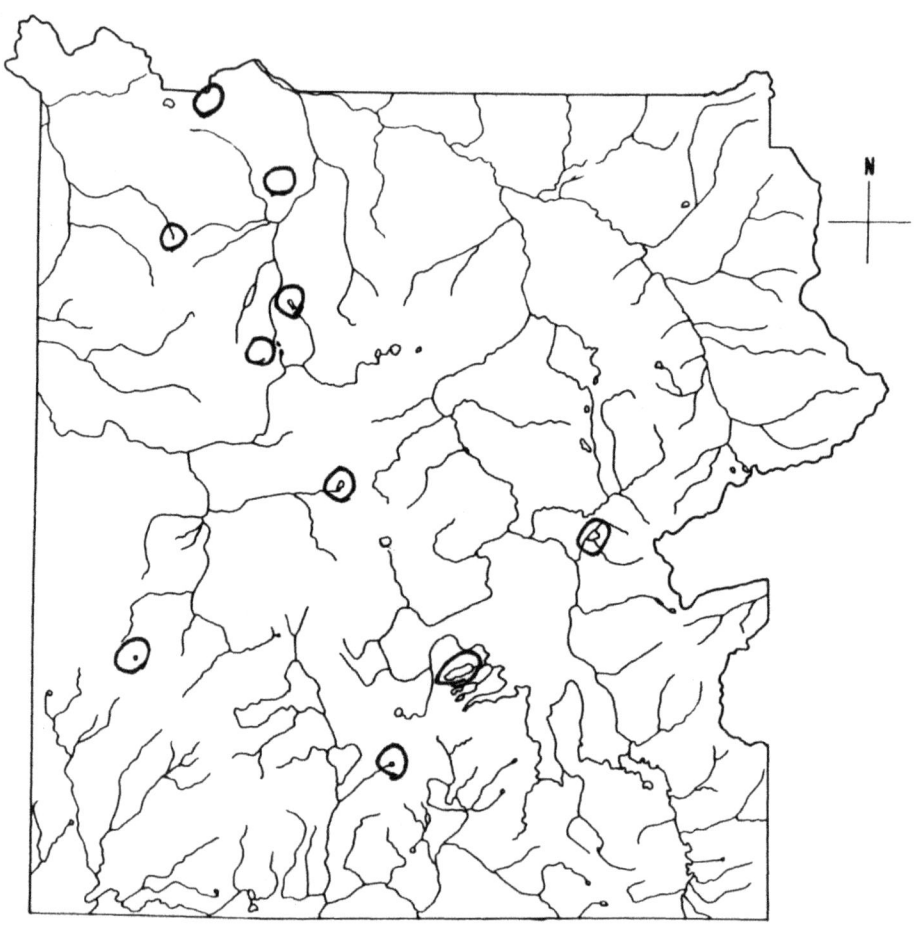

Those waters (circled) in Yellowstone Park that are believed to presently be fishless.

An official fishing trip (2). Left to right: (1) Horace Albright, Superintendent of Yellowstone National Park, (2) Crown Prince Gustav Adolf of Sweden, (4) C. F. Culler, hatchery personnel supervisor, (6) Doug Douglas, the oldest ranger in the park at that time. He came in with the U. S. Army when they were given responsibility for protecting the park. 1926. Tanner collection.

Frank H. Tainter Ph.D.

SPAWN COLLECTION AND FISH CULTURE

The general nature of the fisheries work in Yellowstone Park was to trap fish (originally only from cutthroat) from Lake Yellowstone and some of its tributaries and Fish Lake and take their eggs and milt, fertilize the eggs, incubate them for a short time, and then ship the eggs to other federal and state hatcheries for hatching and for rearing the fish and eventually stocking them in public waters. Some shipments were also made to foreign countries. Later, eggs were also hatched and reared in the Lake Hatchery for directly stocking waters in Yellowstone Park and nearby states.

Fish culturalists were recruited from federal and state hatcheries in Wisconsin, South Dakota, Minnesota, Colorado, Wyoming, Utah, Michigan, North Dakota, West Virginia, Ohio, Tennessee, Missouri, Arizona, Montana, New Mexico, Idaho, and Nevada [1]. Normally, one man was furnished for 60 days by states receiving fish eggs. The experienced men were usually assisted by seasonal college men, or others, for the summer's work.

The pay for temporary employees in 1910 was $1.50 per day for time actually at work [3]. Not withstanding the low wage, there were many applicants for temporary work in the park, as many as one hundred were on file at any one time [4]. Some were willing to work for board only, just for the experience. Political pressures from Washington officials were likely an important influence in final selection. It was not deemed advisable, though, to accept services without compensation. It was Booth's view that everyone should receive the same wages and be expected to perform the same services [4].

Fish Culture in Yellowstone National Park

```
879                TRAVEL ORDER
          TO BE ISSUED BY DULY AUTHORIZED OFFICERS.
                Department of Commerce and Labor
                      BUREAU OF FISHERIES
                          Washington
                                        No. 23 - 13
```

Sir: By authority of order No. 23 of the Commissioner of Fisheries, dated July 1, 1909, you are directed to proceed by the shortest and most direct route from Spearfish, South Dakota to Thumb of Lake, Yellowstone National Park via Gardiner, Montana.

for the purpose of carrying out the instructions hereinafter mentioned, and on completion of this duty to return to Remain at Fisheries Camp, Thumb of Lake and assist in collecting blackspotted trout eggs.

On the presentation of proper accounts you will be reimbursed from the appropriation "Miscellaneous Expenses, Bureau of Fisheries, 1910," subhead "Propagation" for your actual and necessary expenses while engaged as above.

Refer to the number of this order in your account, taking up expenses incurred and upon the face and coupon of each Government request for transportation issued for travel in connection therewith.

Respectfully,

_____ Superintendent.
         (Official title.)

INSTRUCTIONS.

Mr. A. E. Fuller,
    Spearfish, South Dakota.

Sir:

You will please start to-day over the C.B & Q.R.R to Billings, Montana thence over the N.P.R.R. to Gardiner, Montana taking along and delivering to the Superintendent of Yellowstone National Park at Gardiner, 25,000 brook trout

Upon the completion of this work, make out and return messenger and mileage reports and travel vouchers for your traveling expenses during May and then assist Fishculturist Seth M. Ainsworth in unloading and transporting equipment to Thumb of the Lake.

May 23, 1910.

Example of a travel order and work order issued to fisheries personnel. This was addressed to Mr. A. E. Fuller, a permanent employee, detailed to spawn collection in Yellowstone National Park [2].

Previous to 1909, it was possible to assist temporary men with free round- trip passes on the railroad. The cost of a round-trip rail ticket very nearly equaled the total summer's salary if they had to come from another state. So, starting in 1909, each temporary employee was required to pay their own railroad and sleeper fare and meals to and from Gardiner, Montana, and until the party actually started out in the park [5,6]. Booth tried to circumvent the limitation on free passes by sending some temporary men out as assistant messengers with shipments of fish eggs to the park [7]. They would then remain in the park during the season and assist with egg collections.

Each temporary employee was also required to furnish . . . "his own wool bed blankets (five double blankets for each man), towels, sheets, pillows and slips, tarpaulin for bed, oiled slicker, high waterproof leather boots or a pair of hip rubber boots" [8].

Working with temporaries required a great deal of logistical skill to not only select them from a long list, but to make sure that they arrived at Spearfish or Gardiner just prior to departure of the permanent party.

In 1909, the roster of personnel included 23 permanent and temporary workers [9]:

Supt.	D. C. Booth	Spearfish, South Dakota
F. C.	P. M. Stump	Spearfish, South Dakota
F. C.	Glen L. Leach	Put-in-Bay Station

Left July 4

Laborers	A. E. Fuller	Northville Station
	S. M. Ainsworth	Spearfish Station
	Mrs. S. M. Ainsworth	Spearfish Station
Driver	George Smith	

Temporary Laborers
Hod LaBerteu	Bozeman, Montana
Rex LaBerteu	Bozeman, Montana
Tom Fletcher	Billings, Montana
Jack Nason	Sioux City, Iowa
Peter Verdino	Wyoming Fish. Com. Sheridan
Howard Pierce, Jr.	Sioux City, Iowa
Clifford Gorum	Deadwood, South Dakota
Charles Kahle	Deadwood, South Dakota
Oliver Reed, Jr.	Aberdeen, South Dakota

Later Arrivals
Douglas Bradford	Martinsburg, West Virginia
Caldwel Thompson	Martinsburg, West Virginia
Maricey D. Hiliu	Washington, D. C.
Tudar Marsell	Washington, D. C.
George Lancaster	Washington, D. C.
N. M. Gult Nieoh	Washington, D. C.
Mr. Dragstad	Washington, D. C.
Mr. La Mar	Martinsburg, West Virginia

In the 1909 season, Booth, Stump and Leach probably went out sometime in June to prepare for the season's activities. As spawning activity increased in early July, other full-time men along with some of the temporary men arrived. As spawning intensified, the later arrivals would fill in where needed. In this particular year, 1909, Mrs. Ainsworth probably was employed as cook.

During any given season, there were approximately twenty-five people employed—the number having grown somewhat during the 1920s as the Lake Hatchery operation developed and expanded. In 1904, only five men plus a team and driver had comprised the regular work detail at West Thumb ⁽¹⁰⁾. They were later joined by two temporary employees.

As the collection field expanded to Lake and to the east side of Lake Yellowstone in the next few years, more men were gradually added as needed. Some men were sent to Lake Yellowstone for only about six weeks during spawning season, while others were there much longer. *In the mid-1920s, some of the crew from Homer station were detailed to the park for only 2 months (June and July), then back to the Mississippi River for 4 months on fish rescue work (Saeugling). After operational headquarters were moved to Homer, Minnesota, usually four men from the Homer headquarters were the first to arrive. Their duties were to see that the mess house, bunk house and hatchery were in good condition (Tanner).* Naturally, there was a certain amount of housecleaning to be done.

One spring when this crew arrived, they found that the bears had broken into the kitchen, taken a bag of flour and a bag of sugar and spread this all over the floor (Tanner). Their feet were wet from melting snow, and they must have had a dance. The ranger did not know how long this had gone on before he found it and boarded the window shut.

In addition, there were four large boats to be caulked and painted if necessary, and launched, and the spawning and hatchery equipment were to be made ready for use. If any platforms were washed out, they had to be rebuilt before the traps could be set. Within a short time, other men began to arrive in Gardiner by train and were picked up by our truck and brought to the hatchery. By this time, the crew was ready to start setting the fish traps in the streams for spawn taking.

Seasonal employee and Bill Tanner opening up the bunkhouse at Lake Hatchery, 1927. Tainter collection.

Pelican Creek Collection Site, 1925. The men, Cleon Walker in center, are repairing damage from a washout. Note the planks placed on the creek bed to serve as a foundation for rock fill construction of the fish trap. Tanner collection.

A hatchery boat, about to be launched in Lake Yellowstone at the start of the season, 1927. Tainter collection.

NATURAL SPAWNING

This is basically a summary of natural reproduction such as occurs in trout like those which feed into Lake Yellowstone. At spawning time, the trout leave the lake and work their way up into the stream and spawn in the riffles. This is done by a pair of fish working together. They make a depression in the sand and gravel and the female deposits her eggs by twisting her body. The male is alongside the female and goes through the same motion, releasing sperm. If his sperm comes in contact with the openings in the eggs, the eggs are fertilized. By these movements, the eggs are supposed to be buried in the sand and gravel in order to mature. If the temperature is a constant 50° F., the eggs will hatch in about 50 days. The food sacs on the fry, or young fish, will supply nourishment for several weeks. In about 20 to 25 days after hatching, the fry will work up out of the sand and gravel, remain on the bottom of the stream and take some food. In about 30 days, they are ready to swim up into the water. Their first food consists of microscopic plants or animals.

Yellowstone cutthroat trout: female excavating nest, male attending [1].

ARTIFICIAL SPAWNING

Part of the rational for developing the spawn collection and hatchery operations in the park was to reduce natural losses of eggs. Heavy losses of eggs occurred during natural spawning due to severe fluctuations in water level and from predators [1]. At best only 5 or 10 percent of the eggs produced fry.

It was necessary to devise methods to catch the fish as they entered the streams and began working their way upstream. At first, fish were caught by a variety of methods, none of which proved to be very satisfactory as they were labor intensive and did not supply enough eggs to supply the rapidly increasing demand. These included pulling nets behind rowboats in Lake Yellowstone, placing nets across stream outlets, and placing nets in the stream and inducing fish to swim toward the net by slapping the water with tree branches.

During the 1920s, permanent traps became the most common method. Typically, this involved placing or building a wooden platform on the bed of the creek and then placing racks on the platform at an angle to the stream. The slats in the racks were made of 1" by 2" material and spaced about 1" apart. This allowed the water to pass through but prevented the fish from going upstream. In the center of this structure was a V-shaped rack about 18" wide at the back and 2" wide at the front. This structure would allow the fish to pass through the rack from the downside and then go into a holding pen about 8' by 8' constructed of wooden slats. A similar pen of the same size was usually on hand to hold females that were not yet ready to spawn. Both pens were checked daily, and the ready females were spawned. Usually there were about as many males as females and as they were spawned, they were allowed to pass upstream. After the desire for spawning was over, these fish would return to the lake. The usual harvest run of spawning for cutthroat trout was from the middle of June to the middle of July.

Soon after egg collections were begun in 1901 in West Thumb, it was discovered that the relatively remote and inaccessible creeks on the east side of Yellowstone Lake were very productive. The most notable creeks from north to south were: Pelican, Cub, Clear, Columbine, and Beaverdam Creeks [1]. On the west side of the lake were, from north to south: Bridge, Arnica, and Solution Creeks. Grouse and Chipmunk Creeks enter opposite sides of the southern end of the South Arm.

As the Lake Hatchery operations expanded after 1913, fish traps were installed on all these and some other creeks. In addition, a substation was established at Grebe Lake, a small lake from which issues Gibbon River.

Laying beach seine near Clear Creek, 1909-1920 (photo #49,022 – Yellowstone Park Museum).

Frank H. Tainter Ph.D.

Seining at Clear Creek, 1909-1920 (photo #49,023 – Yellowstone Park Museum).

Seining trout at Clear Creek, 1909-1920 (photo #49,030 – Yellowstone Park Museum).

Fish trap near mouth of Arnica Creek, 1936 (photo #49,004 — Yellowstone Park Museum).

Beach seining on Sedge Bay, 1909-1920 (photo #49,028 —Yellowstone Park Museum).

Frank H. Tainter Ph.D.

Rustic hatching troughs and trays for trout eggs, 1909-1920 (photo #49,025 – Yellowstone Park Museum).

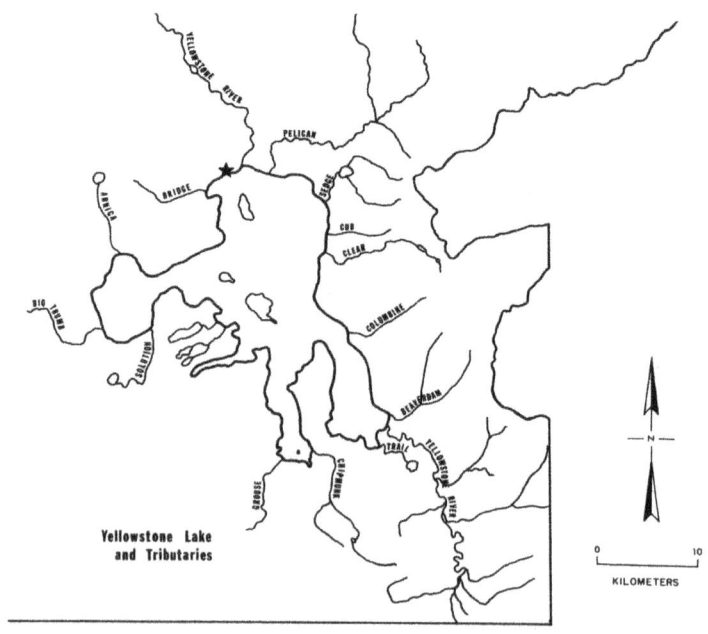

Map of Lake Yellowstone showing major tributary streams and location of the Lake Hatchery (star).

Fish Culture in Yellowstone National Park

SPAWN COLLECTION AT CLEAR CREEK

Upon arrival at the Lake Hatchery in 1925, I met the people who had arrived during the time while I was at the Soda Butte Station (Tanner). Among them were Don Weist, fish culturist on detail from the Leadville, Colorado station, and his wife. They were newlyweds and were to be with me on the work at Clear Creek.

Before the fish began to leave Yellowstone Lake and go into the streams to spawn another crew went ahead to place the fish traps and make any repairs that were necessary. This work was done by boat and the work on Pelican Creek was done by truck. In 1925 this crew consisted of Cleon (Swamp) Walker, Marc Tainter, Les Bennett, and others if necessary.

The following morning, Mr. and Mrs. Weist went aboard the boat with our necessary belongings for spawn-taking at Clear Creek. There were also three men aboard for Peale Island. Our skipper was Roy Ripley from the Charlevoix, Michigan station.

Don's and my duties were to take the eggs from the fish. This work was light at first but gradually increased. We also had to keep the racks on the trap clean. As the snow was melting at higher elevations, there was a heavy runoff of water and a lot of debris collected on the racks. If they were not kept clean, there was danger of a washout; and from 10 a.m. to 10 p.m., it was necessary to clean them hourly. This heavy runoff lasted for about ten days; and after that time, the flow of the creek was back to near normal. The egg production steadily increased, and it occupied about four hours of work each day.

The eggs were kept in about half a dozen ten-gallon wooden kegs. Screens were placed on the tops of the kegs to exclude dirt and small predators. They were then sunk in the lake water where a constant temperature and aeration would be kept until the other boat was ready to pick them up and take them to the hatchery for incubation. The Nautilus would pick up each day's take of trout eggs at three stations and return to the hatchery where the eggs were placed on trays for hatching.

About two weeks from the time we came to Clear Creek, Mr. and Mrs. Weist were taken back to the hatchery where Don was to work in the hatchery and Mrs. Weist was to assist Mrs. Buckmaster, the camp cook, with the meals and kitchen work. They were replaced at Clear Creek by Cleon (Swamp) Walker and Clyde Adams, and we continued to take eggs. Mr. Adams was from one of the trout hatcheries in New England and was a good culturist in all trout work. Walker had three years of experience taking eggs in Yellowstone. Finally, egg taking was finished at Clear Creek; and we removed the racks, trap and holding crates and stored them for later use.

Before finishing spawn taking, a fourth man had been assigned to us at Clear Creek. His name was Lillybridge, and his wife was a very good friend of the wife of one of the officials in Washington. Mr. Lillybridge's health was not good, and he had been granted a six-month leave of absence from his work in Washington. The two wives had been instrumental in getting him a job in Yellowstone. When he was sent over to us, we were informed about his poor health and were asked to not give him strenuous work, to let him get the meals, take care of the cabin, etc. We soon saw that he was not too interested in housework. In a short time, he said he was feeling much better; and he began to tag along with us in our work. The three of us were cutting logs for a new cabin, and he took it upon himself to pile brush. It wasn't long until he did his fair share of all our work.

The logs we were to use were wind-blown lodgepole pine and were located about one-fourth mile from where the cabin was to be built. Many of them were 54' long and not more than 12" in diameter at the butt and 8" at the top. We were now ready to take them to the lake, and this work was all to be done by hand. We opened a trail to drag them there, but they had to be worked through a mixture of fallen timber to get them to the trail. Once this was done, we either dragged or carried them. By this time, Mr. Lillybridge was a full hand and was feeling better by the day.

The logs were rafted together and brought up the lake by a small motorboat to a point near where the cabin was to be built. Again, they were either carried or dragged. Lodgepole pine is rather light compared to some other timber species. Walker and Adams carried the heavy end and Lillybridge and I took the lighter end. We then built the cabin, entirely completing it.

It was getting rather late in the season, so Mr. Lillybridge left us about a week before Adams, Walker and I returned to the Lake hatchery. He had recovered his health and told us that he had never felt better, and that he was going back to Washington to go to work.

Upper Yellowstone River, where it entered Lake Yellowstone, 1927. Tainter collection.

Swamp Walker, Liege Geer, Bill Tanner building a fish trap, 1925. Tanner collection.

Right - Fish trap at Pelican Creek, 1927. Tainter collection.

Lower – Fish trap at Clear Creek, ca. 1930 – Eldon Saeugling and Ray Sampson are cleaning debris from the racks. Both men eventually became fish hatchery superintendents, Saeugling at Guttenberg, Iowa, and Sampson at Homer, Minnesota and Spearfish, South Dakota. Saeugling collection.

Clear Creek cabin, built in 1925. From left: unknown, lad who worked in boat with Roy Ripley, Clyde Adams, Cleon Walker, and Bill Tanner. Tanner collection.

The cabin at Peale Island in 1927, the year it was rebuilt. The cabin served as living quarters for the spawn taking crew, usually three men. Tainter collection.

Rear of cabin at Peale Island, 1925. Gilmer Feustal (left) and Bill Tanner. Tainter collection.

View on Peale Island. Roy Ripley in center. He went by boat from the Lake Hatchery to Peale Island and Clear Creek each day during spawning season to pick up the eggs and take them to the hatchery for incubation. Eggs were transported in the wooden kegs shown in foreground. Tainter collection.

Peale Island in the early 1920s, before the cabin and boat dock were built. Prior to then, the spawn takers lived in tents. Tainter collection.

One of the hatchery boats on Lake Yellowstone, on work detail, ca. 1926. Roy Ripley at wheel, Lester Bennett reclining on deck, Bill Tanner at the bow. Tanner collection.

Hotel and dock at Lake, 1927. The Lake Hatchery was located just to the immediate left of the picture. Tainter collection.

View from dock showing boathouse, left; large excursion boat and smaller fish hatchery launch; fish hatchery; and mess, extreme right, at Lake, ca. 1910-1920. D. C. Booth Historic Fish Hatchery Archives.

An interior setup for a trout hatchery. This is not the Yellowstone hatchery, but the same design has been used since the beginning of trout hatcheries. The troughs are 14' long by 14" wide by 8" deep. The trays for eggs and hatch are made of 1 ½" x 1" frames with oblong mesh wire on bottom. Eggs are placed on the trays and the trays are set into the trough at a slanted position. Usually, one quart of eggs was placed on each tray. Up to 14 trays can be used in each trough up to when eggs become eyed. For hatching, 6 or 7 trays are used per trough. When the fry hatch and start feeding, there are just enough little fish per trough. Tanner collection.

Rearing troughs in Lake Hatchery, 1936 (photo #49,006 – Yellowstone Park Museum).

View showing mess hall (left) and fish hatchery. The crew is loading a shipment of spawn to be trucked to the train station at Gardiner, ca. 1917-1920. D. C. Booth Historic Fish Hatchery Archives.

Interior view of fish hatchery at Lake, showing worker picking dead eggs from trays. Note raceways on right, ca. 1917-1920.
D. C. Booth Historic Fish Hatchery Archives.

Interior view of mess hall at mealtime, ca. 1917-1920.
D. C. Booth Historic Fish Hatchery Archives.

ADMINISTRATION - SPEARFISH

Involvement of personnel from the federal fish hatchery at Spearfish, South Dakota began on May 15, 1901, under the supervision of Superintendent D. C. Booth. Booth entered the park by buckboard and was able to make it through the snow so early because a path had been cleared so that President McKinley could visit the Grand Canyon of the Yellowstone. Exactly how Booth entered into this arrangement is not clear; but in a letter dated July 8, 1912, to Superintendent Thompson, he states that during February 1901, he made a trip to the East with Captain George W. Goode, 1st Cavalry, and Superintendent of Yellowstone National Park, and while enroute the fish cultural possibilities of the Park were fully considered [1]. Capt. Goode took the matter up with Commissioner Bowers and requested that Booth be placed in charge of the work. On March 9, 1901, the Commissioner instructed Booth to correspond with Capt. Goode and arrange for a trip to investigate the streams and waters of the park [2].

During that first season, he was assisted by four soldiers. The U.S. Army also supplied all equipment and provisions. Collections were made only at West Thumb.

From 1901-1909, fish culture activities were limited to the West Thumb area [3]. Spawning trout were stripped and the eggs were eyed in troughs placed in West Thumb Creek and in Yellowstone River near the outlet [4]. The West Thumb station was completed in 1903-4 and enlarged in 1906 and 1912 [5]. A cottage at Thumb for the superintendent was completed in 1908 [6].

Rowboats were constructed and by 1909 cutthroat egg collecting trips were made to Cub Creek and some other east-shore tributaries [7]. Clear Creek was to become a major spawn-producing stream in the

1920s. A small cabin and hatching troughs were constructed there in 1909 or 1913 [8]. During the next four years, the spawn collection operation gradually expanded. Permanent cabins replaced tent facilities at West Thumb.

Difficulties apparently continued to worsen between Booth and higher authorities and in 1912 supervision of the Yellowstone operation was officially shifted to H. D. Dean, supervisor of the Bozeman, Montana federal fish hatchery. Booth was a rather outspoken individual and tended to be blunt or even abrasive in his correspondence. This trait is evident in his correspondence defending the responsibility of the Spearfish station over the spawn collection program in Yellowstone.

As early as 1906, there had been some investigation by the Commissioner of Fisheries into the possibility of the Bozeman station taking over some responsibility of the Yellowstone field station. In 1909, Booth felt a need to defend his position . . . *"The plants of trout made in Yellowstone National Park have been distributed more economically from Spearfish than they could have been made from the Bozeman station . . . The Bozeman station has been unable heretofore to propagate a sufficient number to supply its territory and if so, it is not understood just how it can under such circumstances take care of Yellowstone National Park"* [9].

A month later, Booth defended another apparent encroachment on his territory. In this case, the Commissioner of Fisheries had suggested that Mr. W. T. Thompson, then superintendent of the Leadville, Colorado fish hatchery be apprenticed to Booth for the 1909 field season in Yellowstone.

Booth quickly responded . . . *"This information was received with no little surprise by the writer who regrets that it was apparently thought unnecessary to consult him in regard to the practicability, or even his wishes in a matter involving such a radical departure . . . It is respectfully requested that the office point to one instance in which the writer has erred in his operation of the Park work during the past eight years or where better results have been obtained, . . . It is not understood just how the writer is to 'Go over the ground very carefully' with Mr. Thompson and then report the findings in a joint paper, for Mr. Thompson knows nothing about the field and any paper would very necessarily be written by the writer and he can submit such a paper now as well as later . . . The field is . . . entirely too small for two men with equal authority . . . . It seems doubtful if any good businessman would send two men with equal authority to perform the same errand"* (10).

Booth apparently softened his stance somewhat, as only a year later, he agreed with Mr. Herbert D. Dean's request to turn the field station at Yellowstone over to the Bozeman station (11). During the early development of the spawn collection program in Yellowstone, D. C. Booth had made frequent references to the need for more financial assistance. This, by the way, was a plea frequently made by H. D. Dean and W. T. Thompson when they were superintendents at the Bozeman station and later had responsibility for the Yellowstone field station. In a letter dated March 6, 1911, however, Booth stated rather emphatically that he would not be in charge of the field station in Yellowstone that year (12). Perhaps he acquiesced and did agree to continue for one more year for supervision by the Bozeman station did not begin until 1912. Booth, however, may have used this as a rationalization for outside pressure to transfer jurisdiction in the Park to another station in a letter dated April 20, 1910, to the Commissioner of Fisheries, he complains again about not having enough help and unless he can have some assistance, he would much rather give up Yellowstone National Park (13). He officially resigned his position as superintendent of the Spearfish station to be effective on March 20, 1911 (14).

After he resigned, hard feelings by Booth hindered his administrative capabilities for some time. For approximately a year, S. M. Ainsworth signed all correspondence from the Spearfish station and apparently was the acting superintendent. Booth's whereabouts during that time are not known.

To regress though, the year 1909 was a very active year that was well documented and summarizes some other expenses. In a letter dated March 4 (15), Booth estimated his expenditures for the remainder of the 1909 fiscal year through June 30 at Yellowstone as:

May

Temporary labor, 30 days at $1.50 per day	$45.00
Teams and wagons, 5 for four days at $3.00	60.00
Provisions, groceries, supplies, hay, grain	200.00
Traveling expenses for employees from Michigan	45.00
	TOTAL $340.00

June

Team and wagons, 30 days at $3.00 per day	$90.00
Freight teams and wagons	48.00
Freight on motorboat from Gardiner to Lake	90.00
Provisions, groceries, supplies, hay, grain	250.00
Temporary labor, 200 days at $1.50 per day	300.00
	TOTAL $778.00

Expense of collecting trout eggs at the West Thumb sub-station was:
1901 – 18 ½ cents/1,000
1902 – 19 1/3 cents/1,000
1903 – 19 cents/1,000
1904 – 19 cents/1,000

In addition to the salaries of the permanent men and wages of the temporary help, another expense was for hay for the teams and groceries for the men. The following grocery list was an order [16] placed with the W. A. Hall store in Gardiner, Montana in May 1905 and anticipates that season's needs:

25 lbs. Crackers at 8 cents	$2.00
25 lbs. Peaches at 10 cents	2.50
1 gal. Vinegar	0.40
18 lbs. Butter at 33 1/3 cents	6.00
1 case Corn	2.50
1 lb. Soda	0.10
½ lb. Pepper at 50 cents	0.25
50 cups. Sugar at 7 cents	3.50
27 lbs. Bacon at 14 cents	3.78
½ lb. Flour at $6.80	3.40
1 case Tomatoes	2.40
1 case Peas	2.50
5 gals. Apples at 33 cents	1.65
1 gal. Maple Syrup	1.75
15 lbs. Lard at 11 cents	1.65
¼ lb. Ginger at 40 cents	0.10
25 lbs. Beans at 5 cents	1.25
1 case Condensed Milk	4.50
20 lbs. Salt at 2 cents	0.40
1 lb. Tea	0.50
15 lbs. Coffee at 30 cents	4.50
5 cans Baking Soda at 30 cents	1.50
500 lbs. Hay at $14.00 per ton	3.50
10 lbs. Onions at 2 ½ cents	0.25

6 lbs. Salt at 10 cents	0.60
15 lbs. Corn Meal at 3 1/3 cents	0.50
1 box Matches	0.25
1 doz. Bars Ivory Soap	1.00
5 gals. Kerosene Oil at 34 cents	1.70
4 Camp Kettles at 50 cents	2.00
1 Coffee Pot	0.65
Large Pan	0.65
Wash Basins at 12 ½ cents	0.25
	FORWARD $57.98

A typical day's activities at West Thumb are outlined in the station log for Wednesday, June 16, 1909 [17]:

Supt. at usual duties. Stump seining most all day. Leach assisting with seining and odd jobs. Fuller working on office furniture in a. m. and handling fish in p. m. Ainsworth working on live cans in a. m. Seining over to Duck Lake p. m. Smith in town. Hod & Rex assisting with seining and odd jobs. Fletcher at wood pile working on live cans and odd jobs. Nason assisting with seining, chinking cottage and over to Duck Lake. Verdino assisting at cottage in a. m. and with seining p. m. Pierce and Gorman assisting in kitchen. Kadle working at cottage chinking, etc. Reed assisting Supt. with office work. Seining good but small percentage of ripe fish. Got two live cans made. Found lots of fish at Duck Lake but could not catch them on account of driftwood in the way.

The crew that left last was charged with equipment maintenance. Other needs for the upcoming season had to be anticipated well in advance to be sure they would be available on time. As an example, in a letter dated April 25, 1910, to the American Net and Twine Co., the writer requests a bid on the following equipment for that season [18]:

One (1) seine, 75' long, 10' deep, with bag in middle 20' wide and 20' long, cedar floats, double heavy lead line, double selvage, white No. 16 thread twine, ends ¾" square mesh, bag ½" square mesh.

One (1) Fyke Net complete, double throat, 6' high at mouth, net 18' long, 8 hoops, No. 24 thread white thread, 1" square mesh, each wing 20' long.

Three (3) bags for seine, 10 by 10', No. 16 thread white twine, 1" square mesh (stock pattern).

Six (6) oiled jackets, yellow, sizes 40-42 and 44.

Six (6) oiled pants, yellow, waist 42-44 and 46 inches.

Forty (40) pounds 3/8" American hemp rope.

Six (6) pounds seine twine, assorted, one of No. 6 and 9 hard, the balance from 12 to 16 soft.

One (1) dozen scoop nets complete with 6' handle, 12" hoop, 15" net.

Four (4) oiled soft black hats, size 7 ¼ and 7 3/8.

Four (4) aluminum or white holly wood seine needles.

Four (4) bright steel large sewing needles.

Three (3) gold medal "Easy Folding Chairs", strong, comfortable.

One (1) dozen folding wood chairs, suitable for camp dining room.

The following excerpts from partial camp logs for 1909 and 1910 provide some insight into the season's activities and some of the problems encountered:

June 16, 1909 [19]

- lots of fish in Duck Lake but too much driftwood.
- spent most of time seining.
- used motor-boat for seining.

June 21

- best day for eggs so far, took 64,000 in all.

June 24

- got +100,000 eggs today.

June 25

- completed house today.

June 29

- started getting equipment ready for East-Side. July 1
- proceeding to east-side in rowboat. Stump & Leach still at Lake with boat.

July 5

- wind and waves night before overturned all live boxes and fish were lost.

July 9

- launch was loaded and left for East-Side at 3:30 p. m.

July 14

- the launch had blown ashore the day before, with much damage–picked eggs till 11 p. m. – all hands.

July 22

- Stump took telegram to Thumb

July 25

- worked with photos.

July 26

- Leach arrived at 12:30 noon with provisions and left at 2:50 with provisions and egg cases for Cub Creek.
- apparently got ice at Thumb.

July 27

- Helen went to Thumb 6:30 a. m. and got the army cart to bring ice down. Log of Yellowstone Park West-Side Station for 1910 [20]: June 20, 1910
- Leach, Van Atta, Gay and Sukau go to Lake Hotel to launch boat.

June 22

- Fuller, La Berteu and Mackass made trip around Thumb Bay looking for fish but found none worth working.

June 23

- boat arrived at 10 p. m. from Lake Hotel. June 28
- Leach & Fuller are building a boat – painted it the next day.

July 1

- teams are used to send eggs to Gardiner.

July 2

- Supt. Leach & Fuller went with motorboat to Lake Hotel, thence to Cub Creek with equipment, leaving H. B. Gay in charge at Thumb assisted by Crony and Hargraves – at Cub Creek (about 2:00 p. m.) rough seas and landed in Elk Bay, walking to camp, whole force gathering eggs at Cub and Clear Creek.

July 3, Sunday

- Supt. Booth, Leach, Ainsworth, Mackass, and Dixon left Cub Creek (about 8:00 a. m.) towing live box to Clear Creek and continuing on the South-East Arm of Lake. Seas high and slow progress made after lunch south of Promentory Point, went across and ascended Columbine Creek (seining and collecting eggs enroute, many ripe, unripe, and a few spent fish, a great many males). Camped at S. W. corner of S. E. Arm of Lake.

July 4, Monday

- Supt. Booth, Leach, Ainsworth, Mack and Dixon returned from South-East Arm at 8:00 a. m. Cold morning, overcoats being used on boat. Whole force began early to collect trout eggs from live boxes and seines, securing about 200,000 before dinner. High sea and electric storm at noon continuing until 2:00 p. m. After the storm and when the lake was calm, motorboat made trip to Lake Hotel. Supt. telephoned Major Benson in answer to his call reference to planting trout in Lava Creek on July 3rd.

July 5

- Supt. returned by Hofen boat to Thumb from Lake Hotel.

Log of Yellowstone Park East-Side Station for 1910 [21]:

June 25, 1910, Saturday

- Leach, Cokeley, Ainsworth, La Berteu, Mackau, Urton, Sukau and Williams and wife started for Cub Creek at 5:00 a. m. and arrived at 9:20 a. m. Found things in fairly good shape except that dam was all washed out. Put in day cleaning camp and getting ready to live trap and building dam.

- Leach and Mackau went to Lake Hotel after supplies & returned at night, bring with them W. E. Dixon of Chicago. No seining today, a fine day.

June 28, Tuesday

- Cokeley, La Berteu, Smith and Dixon worked at Clear Creek all day making weir to prevent fish from running upstream. Van Atta, Ainsworth, Mackau, and Washabaugh worked Cub Creek seining and building weir. Urton and Sukau working on dam all day. Made haul at Cub Creek after supper taking about 350 fish. Rained most of p. m. Day's collection 110,000.

July 2

- refer to working in hatchery on East-Side.

July 13

- took eggs p. m., 45,000 at Cub Creek, 47,500 at Clear Creek - bears got into Clear Creek box and helped themselves to about 100 fish.

- Log of Lake Hotel Camp [22] – made camp on lake shore near present site of boat house:

August 1, 1910

- the whole gang cut logs for boat house.

August 2

- finished cutting logs in a. m. and cleaned up boat house site in p. m.

August 16

- were shingling boat house

August 20

- left for Gardiner in morning. Went by wagon. Camped at Upper Basin.

August 21

- went to Norris.

August 22

Norris to Gardiner. August 28

- arrived in Spearfish – after 3 months and 8 days.

Expedition to Yellowstone from Spearfish, 1909. D. C. Booth is in the first buggy. (photo #49,027 – Yellowstone Park Museum).

Camp of expedition to Yellowstone from Spearfish, 1909. D. C. Booth is leaning against tree. D. C. Booth Historic Fish Hatchery Archives.

Boat used on Lake Yellowstone to assist in spawn taking, 1909. This is the same boat as seen on the wagon in photo #49,027 (photo #49,024 – Yellowstone Park Museum).

BOZEMAN

On June 10, 1912, the Bozeman station personnel loaded equipment into three freight wagons, each pulled by a four-horse team [23]. All was loaded onto railroad freight cars at Bozeman and shipped to Gardiner. On their trip into the park, they met heavy snow but were able to maintain three eyeing stations – at Thumb, Lake Creek, and Cub Creek. During June and July, personnel took 29,320,500 trout eggs [24]. Fish spawn collection expanded rapidly during the next decade. Three boats were added in 1912 [25].

The following year, 1913, was especially productive. The spring was much earlier, and spawn operations commenced earlier than usual [26]. The advance men, Mr. Van Atta and Mr. Sleeper of Leadville, Colorado, S. M. Ainsworth of Spearfish, the superintendent, the cook, and several temporary workers left Gardiner May 28 and arrived at noon of the 30th at the Lake Camp.

A hatchery building was constructed at Hatchery Creek, near the north shore of Yellowstone Lake and became the center of the fish culture operations in the park [27]. Additional buildings constructed included a mess hall, dormitories, and a few years later, a superintendent's cottage [28]. Also in 1913, new troughs were constructed, giving a total of 26 double and 2 single troughs, each with eight compartments, 14 ½ x 18 ½ x 8 in. deep, with a normal capacity of seven trays of 9,000 eggs each, or 63,000 to the compartment and over 500,000 to the trough [29].

In addition, a 1 1/2 –story frame building was erected at Clear Creek. This served Cub Creek as well about a mile distant. Temporary troughs with running water were installed there to hold spawn until the boat was able to take them to the hatchery.

The expense of the spawn collection in 1913 is shown in the following [30]:

Blackspotted trout, Yellowstone Park Field.

June temporary labor	$80.22
July temporary labor	250.00
Mess supplies	224.52
Waders and hardware	106.40
Gasoline, oils, etc.	207.74
Team hire and hauling	340.00
Schmauss' salary	60.00
Schmauss' expenses	22.30
Van Atta's salary	125.00
Van Atta's expenses	9.28
Snyder's salary	75.00
Snyder's expenses	101.25
Capell's salary	108.00
Capell's expenses	122.12
Ainsworth's salary	135.00
Ainsworth's expenses	1.85
Superintendent's expenses	30.55

7,446,060 green eggs cost $2,129.23 or $284 per M. Eyeing expenses on above

July temporary labor	$256.80
August temporary labor	63.75
Mess supplies	83.25
Hardware sundries	18.00
Brass egg pickers	4.20
Hauling	170.00

Howe's salary	90.00
Howe's expenses	33.95
Van Atta's salary	25.00
Van Atta's expenses	50.55
Ainsworth's salary	15.00
Ainsworth's expenses	42.90
Superintendent's expenses	7.35
Ice for shipping	14.00

7,009,660 eyed eggs cost $3,003.98 or $0.43 per M. This included packing and delivery at Gardiner, likewise the hatching and distribution of 123,300 of the above eggs into Park waters as fry.

The Yellowstone Park operations expanded quite a bit the following year, 1914, as is seen in the Bozeman station report [31]:

Temporary labor, 1,000 days at $1.50	$1,500.00
Hauling, team hire, etc.	900.00
Mess supplies	750.00
Lumber for Columbine camp, barn and Superintendent's quarters at Lake	700.00
Lumber and hardware for general work	450.00
Nets, seines, and expressage	75.00
Waders, rubber boots and oilskins	125.00
Wire for hatching trays	250.00
Lumber and labor for frames	175.00
Asphaltum, paints and oils	115.00
Galvinized dams	65.00
Tools, appliances, and sundries	125.00
Travel & incidentals for 4 detailed Fish culturists at $175.00 each	700.00
Ice for shipping eggs	40.00

For vessels:

Gasoline, oils, and repairs	$200.00
Material for 14' and 22' hulls	50.00
Freight on above and purchase of engine	150.00
	$400.00

Although spawn collections seemed to be good, a continuing plea beginning earlier when Booth was superintendent and continuing in subsequent reports from Thompson was for increased funding for facilities and for personnel.

Until this time, production from Yellowstone Park was composed almost entirely of eyed eggs that were shipped fifty-two miles by wagon from the Lake Hatchery to the railroad at Gardiner. A major expense was hire of team transportation between the lake headquarters and Gardiner, not only for eyed eggs but for workers, their personal baggage, field equipment, cultural, and mess supplies. Often the teams had heavy loads in one direction but went nearly empty in the other direction.

Part of this loss was alleviated by planning for future developments and hauling building materials when the teams were coming in empty. Advantage was taken of slack times, then, by using these employees on construction work of buildings, dock, and boats.

The authorization to use private automobiles in the park on April 21, 1915 [32] was soon to be a direct boon to the hatchery operations, although as late as 1917, some equipment, supplies, and baggage followed the first trip in on a six-horse trail outfit [33]. At about this time, a 1915 Model T Ford touring car was converted into a pickup truck and was used to ferry personnel and light supplies. *It was also used for maintaining a liaison between the Soda Butte facility and the headquarters at Lake and remained in use at least through the late 1920s (Tainter).*

HOMER

The federal fish hatchery located in the small village of Homer in the southeastern corner of Minnesota on the Mississippi River was built in 1909 and closed in 1952. News reports at its time of closure claimed that it was a pork-barrel project resulting from Congressman James A. Tawney's efforts in Washington, D. C. The appropriation of $25,000 paid for the plot of land and initial construction. It was also erroneously believed that the early purpose of the hatchery was to supply trout fingerlings for stocking of midwestern streams and ponds [35].

However, the hatchery did not begin with fish culture, but rather with clams (Gordon). In 1889, a German button cutter, J. W. Boepple, built a button factory at Muscatine, Iowa. By 1900 that city was said to be the button capital of the world. In the 1890s, an eight-mile stretch of river between Burlington and Clinton, Iowa supported over 300 clammers. In 1899 $66,110 worth of clam shells were sold, making clams the number one fishing industry. Clam beds were productive only as far north as Red Wing, Minnesota, however, because raw sewage from the Twin Cities had spoiled not only clamming but also most fishing.

Flat-bottomed scows carried metal racks with rows of hooks that were lowered over each bed of clams. The clams would be facing upstream with open siphons waiting for food to be carried downstream, but they would mistakenly clamp onto the hook and, thus, be caught. Small operators cooked out their clams, sorted out the various species, and sold them to large operators. A clammer could collect about a ton of shells a day. Shells sold for between $20 to $35 per ton. However, the clamming industry lasted only about twelve years before the beds were depleted.

After complaints began pouring in from constituents about the decrease in the clam populations, the Federal Fish Commission decided to establish several clam stations on the Upper Mississippi River. One of these was at Homer, Minnesota. As the bill was being prepared, pleas by sportsmen's groups encouraged the inclusion of the hatching of fish along with research on clams.

In 1909, 32 acres of partially cleared, gently sloping, river frontage farmland extending from the Mississippi River south to 300 feet past the bluff top were purchased. A large brick house was the only residence on the property. Between 1909 and 1913 three additional houses were built at the edge of the woods for use by permanent employees. The houses were bungalows with broad porches, big windows, and a magnificent view of the river.

Pump house (left), workshop, and the laboratory building under construction at the Homer fisheries station. Gordon collection.

View of the Homer fish hatchery grounds. Gordon collection.

The partially finished laboratory building at the Homer fisheries station. Gordon collection.

Midway down the slope of the hatchery ground a combined office and laboratory building was constructed in addition to a smaller laboratory to the west on the riverbank. The smaller laboratory was for the use of scientists assigned to study the clam problem. Later, an ice-house was also built between two of the ponds.

Visitors were always interested in seeing the vats of hatching trout eggs, agitated by water flowing over a tier of hatching pans (Gordon). One of the duties of the young fish culturists was to pick over the eggs, removing any that were infertile. Fertile eggs become eyed at once and harden up. Infertile eggs soon are infested with a fungus. Walleye and northern pike eggs were hatched in batteries of what looked like glass jugs. These fish, on reaching fingerling size, were shipped out to anyone who had applied for them through his or her congressperson.

In 1900 professors from the University of Missouri established that the larval form of the clams was spent in parasitism on the gills of fish. After three weeks of infection, the larva would drop off, settle on the river bottom, and attach itself to a pebble by a small thread and start to grow.

Now the size of a pinhead, it would take three to five years before it would reach harvestable size. Knowing this, the managers decided to try to inoculate the gills of fish, thus making sure that the larvae had a host. Mr. Surber discovered that not all larvae were receptive to all fish hosts. For example, he found that the larvae of the 'n rhead clam', that produced one of the finest shells, would live only on the skipjack or river herring. After the completion of the Keokuk Dam in 1914, these herrings decreased in number in the upper river, and the number of 'n rheads' harvested was correspondingly fewer.

From 1915 to 1920, both the Homer and La Crosse stations did considerable mussel infection work. Troughs, painted black and covered to keep out light, were used for the bass that were found to be the hosts for the Lake Pepin mucket clam. These two stations at that time were also running fish rescue crews and had plenty of fish to use as hosts. In 1920, the National Association of Button Manufacturers sent seven agents to work with the rescue crews at Homer and they inoculated over six million fish. At that time the shells were averaging $35 a ton and since it cost only $5.35 to grow the shells to marketable size, it was deemed a profitable operation. Later, however, with the change in river conditions, the propagation of mussels was dropped.

When the hatchery was being built, seven large earthen ponds were made by teamsters using scrapers. Intended for use by nest builders such as bass, they were made with one shallow end. This was also handy when the ponds were drained of water and the fish seined out. However, when the ponds were first filled, they would not hold water. Wagon loads of clay were hauled in and tamped down to a depth of 6-8 inches to leak-proof the bottoms. In later years, natural siltation partially solved the problem, but it was necessary for river water to be pumped in from time to time. Bass were introduced, nested, spawned, and flourished.

View of the Homer fish hatchery during construction of the fishponds. In the background horse-drawn scrapers are removing soil from several ponds and in the foreground are several completed concrete ponds. Gordon collection.

Bass were raised for a few years, but it was realized that fish taken from the drying sloughs by rescue crews could fill orders for fish more cheaply than having to raise them in ponds. Thus, the earthen ponds and the dozen or so smaller cement ponds were then used as holding ponds for fish awaiting shipment. In the early years and into the early 1920s, pond "E" at the east end of the station was used to propagate goldfish. They were easy to raise and by September were ready for distribution to anyone with a container.

The westernmost house on the grounds was reserved for use by the superintendent (Gordon). Mr. William Smith was one of the first to live there. On the night of June 26, 1914, the Winona area was struck by a severe wind and rainstorm. At the height of the storm, lightning struck the Smith residence and it burned to the ground. The Smiths were collectors of Indian relics. They had a birch bark canoe in the hallway, lovely Navajo rugs, beaded garments, ceremonial drums, and other artifacts including antique firearms. All was lost. A young Hugh Tainter found a cap-and-ball revolver in the ashes. He replaced the burnt wooden grips, re-tempered the springs and kept it for several years. He left it in the shed at his parents' house and it was buried by bulldozers along with the crushed shed several years later when the main road in Homer was widened.

Government personnel from fisheries stations all over the United States were transferred on detail to the Homer hatchery. For several decades it was the best equipped fisheries station in the country. Two Homer youths started as young workers there and grew up with the hatchery, they were Ray Sampson and Hugh Tainter, the author's father.

The station buildings close to the edge of the riverbank were the brick pump house that housed the pumps that kept the water in the earthen ponds, a maintenance shop, and a boat shed built later in the 1920s. The maintenance shop had a bench running along a row of south windows and was a cheerful place in which to work. All the men who worked there were able to do anything, from using the forge and various machines to make metal replacement parts for broken equipment, to building boats. In 1917 they built the first houseboat to be used in rescue work, the "Margaretta", named after Capt. Culler's daughter.

In 1925, Fritz Drewes, a skilled boat builder from Muscatine, Iowa was sent to the Homer station and placed in charge of boat building. He built a fleet of large cruiser type boats based upon a design of those used on the Great Lakes. About 35 feet long, they could carry three times the load of fish than the earlier scow-like boats, and they had a canopy and side curtains to protect the crew from inclement weather. The dimensions and drawings for boat No. 39 are included in this book. During the most active rescue work, rescue teams used as many as 26 boats and launches and hired over 100 men per season. The total cost in 1917, including salaries for the entire upper river fish rescue project, was $15,000.

View of the fish hatchery at Homer, Minnesota, 1925 or 1926. Note the Yellowstone style motor launches and house boats used in fish rescue work. Tainter collection.

From the years during the First World War to the late 1930s, the main business of the Homer station was fish rescue work. Until the 1930s, when locks and dams were constructed, the depth of the river varied widely. As early as 1878 the Corps of Engineers tried to maintain a 4 ½ foot deep channel. Later, a six-foot channel was maintained by the use of wing dams and piles of rock called rip-rap. That idea was to channel the water current into a relatively narrow channel in the center of the river, but with the "June" rise caused by melting snow further north, the rising water flooded back waters and sloughs, trapping fish.

View of houseboat construction at the fish hatchery at Homer, Minnesota, ca 1930. Tainter collection.

The spring floods that submerged the lowlands along the river channel coincided with the spawning of many fish species that were seeking the quieter backwaters to deposit their eggs [36]. As the conservation movements spread across the United States during the last quarter of the 19th century, and fish hatcheries were constructed to produce fish to stock waters, the idea of saving and utilizing fish trapped in these landlocked pools gained much favor.

Fish rescue work had begun in Iowa in 1878 and steadily grew in volume and importance during the following 60 years. The U. S. Fish Commission started fish-rescue operations in 1889. Although fish rescue work had been extensively done before 1920, this work was given special impetus at Homer in July 1922, when a fund was made available by Congress for the establishment of a special rescue station and permanent personnel [38]. For a time, the supervisor's office was at Homer, Minnesota, but later this was moved to another fish hatchery at La Crosse, Wisconsin. Logistical support, however, remained at Homer throughout the life of the project.

The spawning fish would seek these flooded back waters and when the water went down the hatched fry would be trapped. Later in the summer these waters would evaporate and the fish lost. Although fish rescue at Homer started as early as 1911, 1916 was the first really productive year when 3,324,525 fish were rescued in October and November of that year. In 1921 a total of 176,000,000 fish were rescued through November.

A major problem faced by the U. S. Fish Commission when set up in 1872, was how to quickly move fish from hatcheries to far-off waters throughout the country [39]. Successful experimentation with rail shipments in chilled and aerated water in fish containers encouraged the U. S. Fish Commission to purchase, in 1881, a "fish car" for such shipments. The first fish car was, in essence, a baggage car especially equipped for carrying fish. By 1929, ten special fish cars had been constructed, each bearing improvements to make the handling of fish over long distances more efficient. Car No. 10 had an electric generator to operate all the equipment including the electric aerating devices.

During the 1930s, increased efficiency of motor trucks resulted in their gradually replacing the fish cars. By 1940, only three fish cars were still operating. The last fish car, No. 10, was taken out of service in 1947.

Government Fish Car No. 9. From left: Fred Englehart, captain; Edwin Blosson; a visitor; John Harrington; and Mildred Catte, on step, who four years later married Bill Tanner. Tanner collection.

Ray Sampson and co-worker cutting ice on the Mississippi River near the Homer station. Large quantities of packaged ice were stored in an ice-house and insulated with thick layers of sawdust. Ice was also used in the fish cars for cooling the fish containers. The author recalls that during the summer there was always a tiny stream of cold melted ice water running out on the ground below the ice-house. Tainter collection.

Homer station crew packing harvested river ice in insulated boxes for use in the fish cars. Gordon collection.

The Homer station sent rescue crews out to different areas such as the Hastings to Red Wing section, some to the Wabasha to Winona section. Others worked from Brownsville and on down the river until the fall freeze. The crews lived on houseboats that were towed to the most central part of the assigned area by such launches as the "Tern" or the "Egret". From there the crews went to search out cut-off isolated back waters, seine the areas, transfer the fry by dip net to metal containers, and dump them into the channel or connecting stream. If there were orders for fish to be shipped out, they were taken to Homer by fast launch such as the "Mallard" or the "Avocet", placed in cans and trucked up to a waiting fish car at the Homer train depot.

The "Mallard", the sixty-foot-long launch in which rescued fish were rushed to a waiting fish car at the Homer train depot. Gordon collection.

During the World War I years the government steamer, "Curlew" worked out of the Homer station and served as a base for rescue operations. Fish to be shipped out were held in metal tanks on the first deck.

The U. S. Fisheries steam paddle wheel boat – "Curlew". Gordon collection.

The most significant employee during the life of the Homer station was Clarence F. Culler (Gordon). He began as a laborer at the White Sulfur Springs, West Virginia hatchery and came to Homer in 1918 as superintendent and grew up with the business, so to speak. Through his efforts, in 1922 a special fund was made available for the establishment of a permanent rescue station and personnel. Also in 1922, he was appointed supervisor over all government fisheries from the Alleghenies to the Rockies, and from Canada to the Gulf of Mexico. He left Homer in 1925 when a new office was made available in La Crosse, Wisconsin, and later, in 1940, to St. Paul, Minnesota when the Dept. of Commerce and the Biological Survey were combined into the U. S. Fish and Wildlife Service under the Dept. of the Interior. He died in 1953.

Fay Copper described his experience during the early 1920s working on that expanded program. *All of the physical facilities and equipment such as motorboats, etc. were kept at Homer. During the summer, regular rescue crews operated at Homer, La Crosse, Ferryville, two crews at Lynxville, Marquette, and Bellevue. The reason for the rescue crews was that during the summer, the Mississippi River would be really low and would leave small ponds all over the islands and sloughs. These ponds contained lots of fish that would die if not rescued. After the spring floods subsided somewhat, the rescue crews would go into the backwaters of the river and seine the landlocked fish. Large numbers of bass, bluegills, yellow perch, catfish, etc. were thus rescued. They were collected in cans, transported back to Homer by launch, and then shipped by fish rail cars to points throughout the United States for stocking various lakes and streams. In other instances, the ponds were seined, and the fish were carried in tubs and dumped into the main channel of the river. These fish would have died if they had not been rescued. Fish rescue work ceased in 1936 because of the construction of locks and dams that created a nine-foot channel and control of the erratic flooding that had previously resulted each year.*

With fish raising changing to fish rescuing, the Homer station found itself focusing on boat building and repair business (Gordon). In the late 1930s, the presence of locks and dams on the river then also reduced the need for fish rescue. So, the mission of the station changed quite a bit. A large quantity of quality wood was kept in stock and new boats were built. Also, for a while, large aluminum tanks were constructed for shipment of fish, increasingly by truck. By the late 1940s only a small crew of four men was kept at the Homer station, mostly for vehicle and boat repair. But, much of the equipment was becoming outdated and the cost of repairs was increasing. Also, by this time each station in Region 3 was becoming self-supporting by purchasing their own equipment and hiring personnel to make repairs or fabricate necessary items at the station level.

When the station closed in 1952, Fritz Drewes retired and moved to Winona, Clifford LaLonde was sent to the Great Lakes, Ray Sampson went to Spearfish, South Dakota, and Hugh Tainter to Guttenberg, Iowa. Soon, one by one, most of the remaining stations closed: Lynxville, Marquette, Guttenberg, and Belleview. Only Genoa, Wisconsin is still in operation. Rescue work of a special sort continued at the Guttenberg, Iowa, fish hatchery until it closed in 1968. There, brood stock were netted in the wild and sent to other hatcheries, and specimens were also collected for exhibition at large aquaria in Washington, D. C., the Shedd Aquarium in Chicago, and the Dallas, Texas Aquarium.

During the 1920s, the Homer station had also become involved in the Yellowstone Park fish propagation program. This was at least in part due to the dynamic energy, organizational skill and dedication of Capt. C. F. Culler and he was supervisor of the Yellowstone Park fish propagation project after 1922. During the seasonal fish propagation work in Yellowstone, permanent and temporary employees were sent from Homer and the other stations to assist in that great operation. This had begun as early as 1915 or 1916. The author's grandfather, Frank, and uncle, Marc, were amongst those sent from Homer shortly after that station was established. For these young, and sometimes old, men, and a few women, Yellowstone was, indeed, a wonderous place in which to work.

DEVELOPMENT OF THE FACILITIES

The construction of physical facilities was outlined by Sheldon [1] and Arnold [2]. Highlights are as follows:

1901 – D. C. Booth collected 1,000,000 trout eggs and sent them to the Spearfish hatchery. A hatchery location on Willow Creek was selected.

1902 – A small frame and log building was constructed at West Thumb Creek for the purpose of eyeing eggs there although Booth referred to construction commencing later. In 1903, a building was constructed consisting of two sections, one for the men, the other for egg eyeing and hatching troughs [3]. This was completed in 1904. A camp was set up at Lake.

1906 – A barn and cottage were added to the West Thumb hatchery.

1909 – A small cabin and hatchery troughs were constructed at Clear Creek.

1910 – H. D. Dean, superintendent of the Bozeman federal fish hatchery, collected a few eggs from Fish Lake.

1911 – H. D. Dean took over as superintendent of the Yellowstone fish culture operation.

1912 – Three eyeing stations were maintained in the park – at Thumb, Lake Creek, and Cub Creek [3]. One 16 ft. rowboat and two 20 ft. motor boats were constructed in the park. A speedboat was purchased.

1913 – A new hatchery, the Lake Hatchery, was built at Hatchery Creek, near the north shore of Yellowstone Lake. This building, 34 x 60 ft., was of hewed logs shingled over. It was designed to handle

30,000,000 eggs. The Lake Hatchery became the center of the fish culture operation in the park, a position it retained for the rest of the history of that operation. In order to ensure an adequate water supply, a dam and pipeline were also built. At Clear Creek, a 14 x 30 ft. building with a 10 x 12 ft. ell was constructed. Traps were constructed in the various streams. Previously, fish were collected by use of nets and seines.

1914 – A bungalow and four-horse barn were built at the Lake hatchery. A number of new troughs were constructed to complete the full equipment of 26 double- and 2 single-troughs[4]. Experimental pound nets were also tried for the first time. A 1½ -story log cabin, 14 x 26 ft., was built at Columbine Creek for use of the spawn crew. Spawn collection stations were operated at Lake, Thumb, Clear Creek, Cub Creek, Columbine Creek and Pelican Creek.

1916 – This was the first time that bears caused much trouble. They did a great deal of damage and caused a shortage of eggs [5]. This followed a severe winter. Bears leaving hibernation raided fish traps. Traps had to be removed and fish trapping was abandoned for the season.

1917 – Glen Leach, was field superintendent. He left Washington, D. C. for the park early in July for the purpose of supervising collections of trout eggs [6].

As early as 1917, some eggs were hatched in the park and raised to fingerlings [7]. *At the Lake hatchery, it took about 3 weeks for eggs to hatch; and after the yolk sac was absorbed in 19 days, the fingerling trout commenced to feed on prepared food (beef liver or horse meal), reaching 3-inch length in 1 month, then distributed to park waters (Saeugling). In 1917, 1,773,000 fingerlings were distributed* [8].

Egg baskets were discarded in favor of the tray system for eyeing the eggs [9]. A bulb and glass tube were used to remove dead eggs. Before closing, the workers constructed permanent trap floors and traps on the east side of the Lake [10].

1918 – The Lake hatchery was under the direction of W. T. Thompson of the Bozeman fish hatchery.

1921 - A cabin, 14 x 24 ft., was constructed at Fish Lake by USBF and NPS personnel jointly. This was done to maintain the supply of native trout in the northeastern section of the park [11]. This station, known as the Soda Butte station, had been used for many years as an egg-collecting facility, but without hatching facilities.

1922 – A fish hatchery building was constructed at Fish Lake. Hatching was done there for no more than several years, though, and was then entirely transferred to the Lake hatchery. Charles B. Grates, of Leadville, Colorado, was in charge of the Yellowstone operation this season. 1923 – C. F. Culler, of the Homer, Minnesota federal fish hatchery, was in charge of the Yellowstone operation. The Thumb station was torn down.

1924 – A new cabin was built on Peale Island from the Thumb material. New racks were built at many lake tributaries. The year was very dry, streams were low, and fish formed around the lake margins and did not enter the streams [12]. 1925 – A new cabin was built at Clear Creek. New traps were built on the tributary streams to Yellowstone Lake.

Frank H. Tainter Ph.D.

LIVING CONDITIONS AT THE LAKE HATCHERY IN 1925

We lived in a bunk room over the hatchery (Tanner). There was a large room on either side and a small clothes closet large enough to take care of our belongings. In the center of the room was a large table for our reading or writing with a bench on each side and a chair at each end. There was hot and cold water, a large one-compartment sink with a large mirror over it for our convenience in shaving or washing our hands and faces. A lot of our older fellows used straight-razors and there was a roll of toilet paper by the mirror for them to wipe the lather off their razor blades. Some of us younger fellows were more up-to-date and used safety razors. There were no flush toilets and our JOHN was across the road and up into the woods about a hundred yards. We had gasoline lights that took care of the room very well.

One morning our foreman, Harry Heuver, a bachelor about 50 years old had a call to the JOHN. He was nicely seated when all at once the door swung open and there stood a lady. "Oh!" she said. "I have to go." Harry said, "I will be out soon." She said, "Mister, I can't wait. Is that a two-holer?". Harry said, "Yes." She said, "I'm coming in." Harry jumped up, pulled up his pants and got out of there. When he went by our shop, he went in and told Frank Tainter to take a sign—PRIVATE, EMPLOYEES ONLY— and put it on the JOHN door as soon as he could. We were about ¼ mile from the hotel and went there for our bath—all tubs, no showers at that time. We paid 50 cents for each bath. Our kitchen and dining room were beside the hatchery building and it was constructed of pine logs. On one end of this building were two bedrooms for the kitchen crew. Down the center there was a long table that would seat 30 people. There was a boat company near our place that took in trade. They had two speedboats and a few small motor boats used for fishing or pleasure.

1926 – The otter had increased at Fish Lake and reduced the number of spawning fish.

1927 – The Peale Island station was repaired and re-shingled.
1928 – In October 1926, a sum of $15,000 from William F. Corey of Pittsburg, Pennsylvania, was donated for construction to further fish propagation at Lake Yellowstone [13].

How the money came to be donated for construction of the new hatchery was related by Horace Albright, then superintendent of Yellowstone Park [14].

One day in 1925, William E. Corey, head of the United States Steel Company, invited Albright to his fishing camp just outside the park on Hebgen Lake. Much of the conversation centered on how bad the fishing had become. Albright explained that the little fish hatchery at Lake wasn't adequate to keep pace with heavy fishing being done at that time. When Corey asked what it would cost to build a new hatchery, Albright said, "$27,500." He had requested it from Congress but without success. Just as Albright was leaving the camp, Corey said that he was giving him the money. C. F. Culler, then superintendent of the La Crosse, Wisconsin station, was allowed to match this with federal funds. This money was used in 1928 to construct a number of improvements, the main one being a new hatchery building [15]. This building was of frame and log construction and 48 x 108 ft. It contained an office for the hatchery superintendent; a main room 48 x 68 ft., which was devoted to hatching and packing eggs and fish for transportation; and an aquarium in which native fish were exhibited. There was a balcony overlooking the main hatchery room where attendants working with the fish and eggs could be viewed by visitors. Its capacity was estimated at 25 million or more eggs per year.

Horace Albright, then superintendent of Yellowstone Park, offers an interesting anecdote as to the selection of the site for this hatchery [16]. Secretary of Commerce Herbert Hoover visited the park in July 1927 and stayed at the Lake Hotel. Albright had invited Hoover and C. F. Culler, superintendent of the present small fish hatchery at Lake, to supper. After supper, they walked the mile to the site of the old hatchery. Culler explained why he thought the new hatchery should be built right alongside the old one. Albright felt that the new hatchery should not be built on the lakeshore, but up the road a little way and out of sight. After asking questions and walking around a bit, he announced his decision by placing his walking stick in the ground in the middle of the site that Albright favored.

In addition, three new rearing ponds were built on Hatchery Creek about 75 yds. west of the new hatchery building. These were 118 ft. long, 106 ft. long and 98 ft. long and 5 ft. wide. Previously, fish were planted directly from the hatchery that often resulted in serious losses. With the new ponds, young fish could be held and fed before they were planted in park waters. Construction of new rearing ponds was started at Mammoth [17].

In 1928 Hugh Tainter and Roger Tanner hauled wooden pipe from the railroad station in Gardiner to replace the old water line to the hatchery and helped install this line. A small pond at the source had a fence around it to keep wild animals out of the water. Hauling the pipes from Gardiner to Lake was a thrilling experience.

We could have safely hauled a few pipes at a time, but this would have taken forever since there was a total of one mile of pipe to be transported (Tainter). We used two fisheries trucks and an old NPS truck and loaded them to capacity. The 1925 Dodge truck I drove was a good tough truck but the 4-cylinder engine did not have enough power or the transmission sufficient gear reduction to carry the load up some of the steeper slopes. As the truck would begin to stall, I would step on the clutch pedal and simultaneously lock the rear wheels with the hand brake. Then I would rev up the engine, pop the clutch, disengage the hand brake, and the truck would jump ahead a few feet. Because of the overloaded condition caused by the long pipes, the front end of the truck would rear up off the ground then bounce back to the ground with a jolt. I eventually worked my way up the hills. This may seem awfully abusive of the truck but since I was the mechanic of the cars, trucks, and boats, I knew that this truck was well-designed and could stand the abuse. Besides, we had no other choice but to get the job done any way we could. This independence almost got me into trouble on several other occasions.

Once I took some trout fingerlings to stock some small lake in the Central Plateau. On my way back I stopped for lunch near Sulphur Mountain. I built a small fire to heat my lunch and realized when I was finished that I could not extinguish the fire. Every time I would step on it, embers would explode, and several new fires would start. I had a tough time finally extinguishing all the fires. When I later mentioned this to one of the rangers, he laughed and said that that old road was once used by tourists but because of the danger of catching the sulphur on fire it was closed off and no longer used.

The main roads in the park were in reasonably good shape and were sprayed with an oily substance to control dust. Because of the oil, the roads could become extremely slick. Since the roads were often filled with tourist cars, the Park Service enforced strict speed limits over all vehicles. The hatchery personnel were oftentimes hard-pressed to get all their work done, especially when hauling fish eggs from Lake to the railroad station in Gardiner and observe speed limits. As a result, a game of wits was often played between them and the road patrolmen on their motorcycles. As mechanic for all the cars, trucks, and boatmotors, I had the best job in the park. I had a different job every day, often hauling eggs to Gardiner, returning with supplies. In 1929 I hauled back all the glass sheets for the new aquarium at Lake. I hauled one of the 35 ft. Great Lakes style cruisers from the railroad station in Gardiner to Lake. The four boats used there had been constructed by my father, Frank, myself, and others at the Homer station. They were of a design with modeled hull and high bow to safely withstand the high waves that could occur on Lake Yellowstone during storms. There were also frequent visiting dignitaries and it was my job to show them around.

Once when I was driving the truck to deliver goods, Superintendent Horace Albright asked if he could ride along (Tainter). Later when we were driving on a road next to the Grand Canyon of the Yellowstone River, I noticed that the truck was drifting toward the canyon's edge. When I tried to correct, nothing happened! I hit the brakes just as the truck went off the road and down the slope. Fortunately, the truck was stopped by a huge cluster of bushes. I discovered that a bolt holding on the pitman steering arm had fallen off and was lost. I removed a bolt from the truck bed and was able to cobble together a repair. Later Superintendent Albright said *he would never forget the expression on my face as the truck headed for the canyon's edge.*

1929 – The Lake Hatchery was completed. The ten new rearing ponds at Mammoth were completed.

A new bunkhouse was also built at Lake, containing 15 individual rooms 9 x 9 ft., equipped for two men in each room. The entire building was 27 x 86 ft., containing a recreation room 15 x 24 ft., one bathroom 9 x 15 ft. with two showers, 4 basins, and one toilet. The new mess house was 24 x 56 ft., with a large dining room, kitchen, pantry, and living quarters for the cook [18]. A new sewage disposal plant was also constructed and the boat dock was rebuilt and extended. Artificial feeding of hatchery-reared cutthroats became popular at about this time [19]. Oatmeal, salmon egg meal, horse meat, and various parts of hogs, sheep and cattle were fed. This never became very successful, though, as lack of space and high costs prevented large-scale fish feeding and was largely discontinued at the Lake hatchery by 1932. The ten new rearing ponds at Mammoth were completed [20]. The ponds were of wood with clay-filled walls and bottoms. They were to have a capacity for 250,000 large trout. The ten 75 x 4 x 5 ft. trout rearing ponds were located at Mammoth for several reasons. Firstly, there was an unlimited supply of water. Supplementing this with runoff from Mammoth Hot Springs allowed temperature control so that the ponds could be used year-round. It was the intention to produce several thousand fingerlings each year that would be planted in the more accessible streams rapidly fished out early each season.

1930 – A 14 x 20 ft. log living quarters and feed room were built at the Mammoth facility for the preparation of fish food. A garage 80 x 24 ft. was constructed about 100 yds. north of the hatchery building [21]. It contained two rooms 9 x 11 ft. each, on one end and used for storage, and a workshop 21 x 34 ft. on the east end of the building, with room for seven cars and trucks. Heavy fish losses were experienced at the Mammoth facility [22]. Poor water quality and extreme temperature fluctuations caused a number of diseases. The raceways collapsed in

1931. Creosote applied to wooden intake water pipes in 1930 and 1932 also caused losses. The station was a failure and was abandoned in 1934.

Fish trap at unknown location in Yellowstone Park. Saeugling collection.

Hatchery personnel in 1924. Seth Ainsworth was in charge of the station that year. Front row on left: (1) Lester Bennett, Mrs. Ainsworth, (4) Marc Tainter, Roy Wagner reclining. Second row: Cleon Walker on far right, Frank Tainter next to him with tie. Tanner collection.

Hatchery personnel in 1926. The Clear Creek and Peale Island crews are not present in this photograph. From left, front row: Mrs. Bushmaster, (5) Alice ?, (6) Archie Capel, (7) Frank Tainter, (8) Cleon Walker. Standing, from left: (2) George Eisenlohr, (3) Harry Heuver, (6) Roy Ripley, (7) L. Geer, (8) Edward Hill, (9) Lester Bennett, and Mr. Robinson. Tanner collection.

Hatchery personnel, in 1928 or 1929. The Gardiners and Ryans (cooks) are seated. From left: Harry Carson, Jimmy Banner, Al Anderson, unknown, Eldon Saeugling, Les Bennett, Ted Feustel, unknown, Dick Fenucan, Hugh Tainter, George Eisenlohr, Cal Ryan, Ed Johnson, Bill Tanner, Harry Heuver (in front), Jack Bunch (behind Heuver), John Gardiner, Fielding Tainter, and Frank Tainter. Tainter collection.

Camp at Fishing Bridge, 1925 or 1926. Roger Tanner on left and two seasonal employees. Tanner collection.

The old Lake Hatchery building (left) and mess hall, built in 1913, as photographed in 1927. To the far left is seen a portion of the boat house which is still in existence. Tainter collection.

Frank and Hugh Tainter at railroad depot in Gardiner, with Graham Brothers truck and a load of wooden conduit for LakeHatchery, 1928. Tainter collection.

National Park Service truck (note hard rubber tires) loaned to Bureau of Fisheries and used to haul wooden conduit from Gardiner to Lake Hatchery. Hatchery mess hall is in background. Hugh and Frank Tainter are standing on either side of rear wheel. Tainter collection.

Hauling conduit for the new water supply at the Lake Hatchery, 1928. The truck has reared off the ground because of the tail-heavy load. Drawing by Roxanne Chase.

(Right) Water supply pond for Lake Hatchery, 1928. Tainter collection.

(Lower) Hugh Tainter just after hauling in boat from Gardiner, 1927. He and his father, Frank, have started setting up the blocking to assist in unloading the boat and launching it in Lake Yellowstone. Tainter collection.

Lake Hatchery boats and dock, in 1924. Tanner collection.

Lake Hatchery dock and the three 35' Great Lake style cruisers, 1928 or 1929. Tainter collection.

The Lake Hatchery boat dock, during the visit of President Calvin Coolidge to the facility, in 1927 (2 photos). Tainter collection.

New fish hatchery at Lake, 1929 (2 photos). Tainter collection.

(Right) View of rear of new Lake Hatchery building, 1929. Tainter collection.

(Below) New fish hatchery at Lake, under construction in 1928. Haynes Picture Shops, Inc.

New bunkhouse at Lake, under construction in 1928, with construction crew. Haynes Picture Shops, Inc.

Trout rearing ponds at Mammoth Hot Springs, 1929 (photo#49,048 – Yellowstone Park Museum).

FISH LAKE AND THE SODA BUTTE STATION

Fish Lake (or Trout Lake as it is now called) is a small lake of about 3 acres located in the northeastern corner of the park, a few miles from the Soda Butte landform. A combination of factors has caused this lake to be unusually productive, a fact that was early recognized by park visitors, administrators, and poachers.

The outlet from the lake is on the southeast shore of the lake. As the water left the lake, it flowed over a natural rock ledge and from there into Soda Butte Creek about ½ mile away. *The low dam presently located at the outlet was not there in the 1920s (Tanner) but could have been placed there after the lake was drained to remove the cutthroat trout during the late 1930s.* During the latter part of the last century, Fish Lake contained a dense growth of vegetation [1] and supported a large population of fish. The abundance of trout inhabiting this lake was noted as early as 1878 when an Army surgeon, Dr. S. Weir Mitchell, was amazed when soldiers of his party's escort were able to take trout weighing five pounds in such numbers as to nearly swamp their raft [2].

Water flowing into the lake is of the magnesium bicarbonate type, the rarest water type in Yellowstone, and perhaps in North America [3]. *The water flowing into Fish Lake was very tasty and very soft (Tanner).* This class of water is most commonly produced from dolomite rocks that have a strong magnesium component. Only two other such lakes in Yellowstone (Foster and Gallatin) are of this type [4].

The productive nature of this lake and its large trout were an important item in the diet of the residents of Cooke City, who were accustomed to taking fish there with powder, spear, and seine [5]. On one occasion, Park Assistant Fish, with Cassius Conger, the superintendent's son, found a man in the vicinity of the lake carrying a fish spear and later heard that 80 pounds of fish were brought into Cooke City [6]. By 1886, poaching of fish and game was so extensive that a detachment of U. S. soldiers was stationed there [7].

Trout in some park waters were parasitized by worms that were viewed upon by revulsion by many anglers. It was noted, however, that the fish in Fish Lake were free of parasitic worms and this may have further enhanced palatability of fish from its waters.

The productivity of Fish Lake may also have sparked the idea for some of the first stocking in the park. In 1881, Superintendent Norris[8] transplanted 10 trout and numerous eggs from a "particularly productive lake" (probably Fish Lake) into various barren lakes and ponds nearby.

Cutthroat trout eggs were first taken from Fish Lake in 1910 [9], nearly a decade after eggs were taken first collected at the West Thumb hatchery. That year the Bozeman, Montana, hatchery began egg collection in the park at Fish Lake with the entire operation turned over to that more convenient hatchery the next season. The Fish Lake site was known as the Soda Butte Station. High productivity coupled with being more than 1000 feet lower in elevation than Yellowstone Lake allowed earlier accessibility in the season and earlier spawning undoubtedly continued to its eventual rapid development.

Collections at the Lake hatchery facility usually did not commence until sometime after early June because either the Lake road was impassable because of deep snow [10] or the streams were still filled with ice [11]. In 1927, 10 miles of road between Canyon Junction and the lake were almost impassable because of several washouts from heavy snowfall [12]. The road to Soda Butte and on to Cooke City had heavier use and also had less of a tendency to become drifted shut by blowing snow. When C. F. Culler arrived May 22, 1923, at Gardiner to assume charge of the fish-culture operations in the park [13], he went with his crew first to the Soda Butte station for the first egg collections. *Fish Lake was loaded with natural food for the trout (Tanner). There were millions of freshwater shrimp, which were about one-inch long and as big as a pencil. There was decayed vegetation on the lake bottom at that time of year. In those days, the fish in this lake were larger than those in Yellowstone Lake, about 16 to 18 inches in length while the ones in Yellowstone Lake were 14 to 15 inches.*

REMEMBRANCES OF FISH LAKE

My first fish culture work in Yellowstone began in 1925 and was with Mr. Buckmaster, a well-known and well-trained foreman and fish culturist on detail from the Spearfish, S. D. station (Tanner). We were at the Soda Butte unit located at the northeast corner of the park near the Soda Butte ranger station, and just off the road leading to Cooke City, the end of the road at that time. We were housed in a one-room cabin on about a three-acre lake. Our purpose was to set up the hatchery for operation, install the trap in the small stream leading into the lake, take eggs from the fish that came into the trap, and incubate them in the hatchery, and the remainder were planted in small streams nearby. The method was to open up sand and gravel beds, place the eggs in them, then recover the beds with the sand and gravel, and in due time the little fish would hatch, work themselves out, and be on their own.

Mr. Buckmaster had done well in training me as a spawn-taker and in teaching methods of handling the eggs, the fish trays and hatchery procedures. We were almost finished taking eggs as Soda Butte lake water was a little warmer than that of Lake Yellowstone. This little lake was a good producer of eggs as well as food life for the fish in it. It is off the main road and in 1925 one had to walk a half a mile to reach it, so that explained the good supply of brood fish in it.

After getting chores done for the day, I found that I had quite a bit of time for myself and I liked to use it watching the wild animals around us. There was a colony of otters at the lower end of the lake. Their best performance was at daybreak. I also played hide and seek with an antelope. Regardless of how early I went out in the morning, it was around. I would always get back to the cabin for breakfast and sometimes I would have to get Buckmaster up. Then he and I worked in the hatchery and took eggs and then I was free again for the day. By this time a herd of elk, about 15 of them, had moved down from the timber onto the flat land to graze on the new grass. There was a big flat rock near our cabin that I could work myself onto without the game seeing me, and I could watch them. The cow elks always kept a lookout for poachers, and more than once I saw one putting a coyote over the hill.

On one occasion I saw a mother antelope giving her baby its breakfast. I watched them until she bedded the baby down, then I started to walk over to get a good look at it. As I approached, the mother became very lame, attempting to coax me away, but I kept my eye on the spot and moved on. When I reached it, the mother was very close and could hardly move. Now she was crippled in two legs. The sagebrush was very dense and you can be assured that I did not find the baby. When I retreated, she began to improve and loped away. We had a colony of beavers that were interesting as they built their dam. Also, there were badgers and prairie chickens.

I knew the nearby Park Ranger, Jimmy Dupuis, a French Indian. His was a one-man station, and his duties were to see that the buffalo did not work out of the park at that point. He had a saddle horse and a pack horse. He told me one day that he would like to have me go along on some horse patrols, but he was sure the pack horse would not carry me because he bucked and had thrown him a few times when he tried to ride him. But his young son, about twelve years old, would ride him anywhere and it never bucked with him. So, we went out to look the horse over and I gave him a chew of my smoking tobacco that he apparently enjoyed. Then we put the saddle on him and I crawled on his back. About that time, he made a lunge and I was off. I gave him another chew of tobacco. I made a few trips with Jimmy and I rode his pack horse bare-back and fed him my tobacco. In this way we got along fine, and whenever we would stop and I was off of him he would nudge me for another chew. About this time school was out in Livingston, Montana and Jimmy's wife, daughter, and son joined him for the summer. The young son took over riding the pack horse, so my enjoyable trips with Jimmy were over.

About three weeks after I went to Soda Butte, our supervisor, Mr. Culler, came in one afternoon with a young lad for my replacement and advised that Clear Creek on Yellowstone Lake was in need of another spawn-taker, and I was to get ready and go back with him.

For personnel stationed at Soda Butte, the place was rather isolated. In 1925 and 1926 we could get within ½ mile of the cabin and hatchery with a truck. Our supplies were unloaded and we packed them in from there, same for anything coming out, including the eggs that went to the Lake hatchery. There was a bus (stage) that ran from Gardiner to Cook City (end of the road). Early in the season the bus made three trips per week, as times got better it ran every day. We had a good-sized wooden box down by the road with a sign on it (U. S. Fisheries). Inside was a cloth bag tagged U. S. Fisheries, Soda Butte, in which we would put our mail. The bus driver would leave the mail in this box. We also had a bag for the grocery store in Gardiner. The driver handled this the same as the mail. We were never short one cent, or lost anything. The driver advised me there was no charge for his service, that he did it for all of his good friends along his route.

The Fish Lake site was used for egg collecting for many years, but without hatching facilities. Fish traps were constructed in 1919. Initially the workers lived in tents, but construction of a new hatchery building was begun on May 29, 1922 [14]. It replaced a small, temporary log structure and allowed egg hatching to be done. *Although the station there had the troughs and trays and could have taken care of at least 100,000 fingerlings up to 2 inches in size, in 1925 and 1926 at least, only egg taking was done (Tanner).* The Soda Butte Station was operated as a branch of the Lake hatchery.

Spawning at Fish Lake began as early as May 7 and lasted as late as July 15 during the period 1929-36 [15]. The average run lasted approximately 27 days, with a maximum of 45 days in 1932 and a low of 12 days in 1930.

Egg collections of cutthroat trout gradually increased during the 1920s to reach an average of approximately 1.5 million taken annually 1919-37 [16]. By 1929, though, the net contribution of Fish Lake (.864

millionths of 14.1499) to the entire production within the park was overshadowed by some streams flowing into Yellowstone Lake, including Chipmunk (2.914), Clear (1.169), Cub (1.289), Grouse (3.145), Pelican (3.3107), and Thumb (1.296). A weir was installed in the Buck Lake inlet stream in 1939 and 101,000 cutthroat eggs were collected [17].

In 1934, it was decided to remove cutthroats from Fish Lake and restock with rainbow trout. The latter species was stocked in 1935 and a few spawn rainbows were trapped in 1936. Any spawn that visually appeared to be cutthroat or rainbow x cutthroat hybrids were removed from the lake. By 1940 the lake's population was pronounced as "pure" rainbow trout [18]. An average of 621,000 rainbow eggs were trapped from this brood annually during 1937-50 [19]. In retrospect, it appears that although these were pronounced to be pure rainbow, they were almost certainly rainbow x cutthroat hybrids similar to the present fish in the lake [20]. Traps were removed in 1950 and the station turned over to the National Park Service in 1951.

Fish Lake, and mountains beyond in the southeast, photo taken from the north shore, 1927. Tainter collection.

The bunkhouse at the Soda Butte Station, 1927. From left to right are, George Freise, Hugh Tainter, and Roy Anderson. Tainter collection.

Hugh Tainter, by pile of antlers in front of cabin at Soda Butte hatchery, 1927. Tainter collection.

THE BOATS

Soon after egg collections were begun in 1901 in West Thumb, it was discovered that streams on the east side of Yellowstone Lake were very productive. In all, a dozen or so streams were continuously trapped.

Following collection at each stream, the eggs were kept in about six ten-gallon wooden kegs. Screens were placed on the tops of the kegs to prevent anything from getting into them. They were then sunk into the lake where a constant temperature and aeration would be maintained until the boat arrived to pick them up and take them to the hatchery for incubation. This was done daily.

From 1901 through 1909, fish culture activities were limited to the West Thumb area [1]. Rowboats were the only watercraft used to assist in collection at nearby streams, although a medium-sized trunk cabin cruiser was freighted in by horse drawn wagon in 1909.

Specifications for that cabin cruiser were [2] . . . "28 ft. long, beam 7 ft., 10 H. P., two cycle, two cylinder engine, ten port and dead lights two on each side hinged, name in polished brass, also number, galley provided with two burner gasoline stove, commissary storage, ice locker, toilet room fitted with cruiser type yacht closet with necessary connections and self-closing brass valve, floor covered with good grade linoleum, seats provided with cushions covered with leatherette, top of cabin reasonably strong to support any weight, polished brass rail 4 ½ inch high to extend around the after deck, cockpit covered with standing roof with drop curtains and glass shield hinged to connect top of standing roof and cabin in order to protect engineer, ten streamlined life preservers, fifty-pound anchor and fifty feet of heavy manila rope, closed cabin and cockpit provided with seats covered with cushions, the seats in closed cabin to be hinged and made to extend so as to be used for berths."

This boat was constructed by the Truscott Boat Manufacturing Co. of St. Joseph, Michigan, and delivered to Gardiner, Montana for a price of $1,426.00 [3]. It weighed approximately 4,500 pounds. It was identified as U. S. Fisheries No. 8 [4]. In addition, a 16-ft. long rowboat was also purchased and shipped with the cabin cruiser [5]. It cost an additional $36.00 and weighed 225 pounds.

In 1912, four more boats were added. One 16' rowboat and two 20' motorboats were constructed in the park and a speed boat was purchased.

The following year, the operation was moved to the new hatchery at Lake and, subsequently, was greatly expanded. Reliable transport of eggs from the stream collection points to the hatchery was a continual problem as the boats were small and could not carry the combined daily output of eggs from the collection sites. In addition, heavy waves during storms forced postponement of some collections and loss of eggs. In 1914, two boats were constructed at Lake, of 14' and 22' lengths. Even larger boats, however, eventually were brought to Yellowstone and successfully used after administration of the program changed in 1922 to the federal fish hatchery at Homer, Minnesota

The federal fish hatchery at Homer, Minnesota was the center of a massive fish rescue operation in the upper Mississippi River. Spring floods would submerge lowlands along the river channel. Spawning fish would seek out these quieter backwaters to deposit their eggs [6]. As the river level fell, these fish were trapped in the landlocked pools and died as the pools dried up. The fish were rescued by seining and were either placed back into the river or shipped to other parts of the country for stocking of rivers or ponds. This necessitated fast boats that could carry a large number of containers in which to transport the living fish to the rail head.

A boat design popular to that time and used by Great Lakes commercial fishermen was adopted for this use. Boat builders at the Homer station constructed several of these for use in the fish rescue work. When the Homer station was made the headquarters for the

Yellowstone spawn collection program in 1922, it was only natural that the usefulness of these boats was recognized.

During the next 30 years, at least four of these boats were used on Lake Yellowstone. The boats were about 33-35' long, had modeled hulls and high bows to safely weather the heavy waves that could occur on Lake Yellowstone during storms. The 28 pairs of ribs were of steam-bent white oak. Planking was of cypress. The large house roof provided protection from rain. Although the sides were open, canvas tarps could be lowered and snapped into place to provide protection from wind-driven rain and cold winds. At least one of these boats was later fitted with glass panels and was probably used more extensively for research purposes and for ferrying visiting dignitaries.

Careful study of photographs reveals that the four boats differed in minor details and slightly in overall shape. A crew of 3-4 men was employed at the Homer station to build watercraft of all sorts. These crafts ranged from simple rowboats, to cruisers, houseboats, and even entire towboats and barges. The men were highly skilled craftsmen who were also very pragmatic, and they developed a number of time-and labor-saving shortcuts that eased their work considerably. For example, that portion of each rib with severe curvature was sawn lengthwise to shorten time and ease bending. Hot-dip galvanized carriage bolts were used extensively to hold things together. A good job of caulking would tighten the whole boat and make the hull sound like a drum.

The boats were shipped from Homer, Minnesota to Gardiner, Montana by rail, unloaded, and then hauled by truck 54 miles overland to Lake. Their identification numbers were: 8, 39, 40, and 54. At least one was also known as Nautilus. Boat number 54 was affectionately known as old "54". The fate of two of these boats is unknown. No 54 was shipped back to the Midwest in 1939 and used in the construction of the federal fish hatchery at Guttenberg, Iowa, and retained for use there until condemned in the late 1940's. The hull was sold to a man from Davenport, Iowa for $10.00. It was powered by a Model 35 Kermath marine engine. This engine was in possession of the author, having been acquired by his father when the boat was condemned. This engine is presently in the restored boat No. 39 in the D. C. Booth Federal Fish Hatchery Museum in Spearfish, South Dakota. At least two of these boats were powered by Model 35 Kermath engines.

During the course of research on the fish spawn collection activities in the park, it was learned that one of these old boats was still in existence in a rather dilapidated condition, in private ownership in Corwin Springs, MT. Judging from an examination of photographs, it is probably No. 39. Since this boat was privately owned and its future uncertain, and since it was used during a unique part of Yellowstone's history, it was decided that its measurements and lines should be preserved. The original plans were known to be in existence as late as 1954 but evidently were subsequently discarded. Examples of this once popular design are rare today.

Some major length and cross-sectional measurements were obtained and were used to construct a half-hull model from which missing measurements were derived. Details were provided by study of old photographs of all the boats and from numerous photographs taken of the existing boat. Several sets of working drawings were produced, each one more complete, until a final set of working blueprints was produced. A 1 1/8" to 1' scale model was constructed for the fish hatchery museum being planned for the Lake hatchery site. These plans were not funded, however, and the model is presently in the D. C. Booth Fish Hatchery Museum in Spearfish, South Dakota.

Frank H. Tainter Ph.D.

THE WAY THERE

Previous to 1915, the major overland transportation to Yellowstone Park was the Northern Pacific railroad. Hatchery personnel from the Spearfish, Bozeman, Homer, and other federal fish hatcheries would travel to Gardiner by train. Then, they and their baggage and supplies were transferred to freight wagons for the arduous trip to West Thumb or Lake. Fish eggs would be hauled out by team by the same route for shipment by rail from Gardiner.

The authorization to use private motor vehicles in the park on April 21, 1915 [1] was soon to be a great boon to the hatchery operation. As late as 1922, when Clarence Culler became supervisor of the Yellowstone spawn collection and hatchery operation, he and some seasonal employees still journeyed by train to Gardiner. The majority of permanent employees, however, drove out in government trucks, carrying with them supplies that would be needed during the forthcoming field season.

After 1915, and through the 1920s, the major, and for a long time the only, thoroughfare from the eastern states to Yellowstone was a series of trails loosely connected into much of what eventually became known as Highway 12. Earlier, in 1911, a "pathfinder crew" sent by the Minnesota Automobile Association worked out this combination of trails as a practicable route to Yellowstone from the Twin Cities [2]. This primitive route became known as the Yellowstone Trail and later was identified by orange symbols the size of a pie plate painted on rocks, trees, telephone poles, and barns [3]. *A, Y, or P (Atlantic, Yellowstone, and Pacific) were the only highway markers in the mid-1920s (Tanner). Those letters were painted on rocks, bridges, trees, or on anything else along the road that could be used.* Later, the Yellowstone Trail was extended to both east and west coasts.

In the 1920s, though, there were few signs and no road maps to speak of. Although the crews from the Homer fish hatchery might follow any one of a series of trails, the preferred route was to leave the Homer station, drive across Minnesota always working in a northwesterly direction until the Yellowstone Trail was intercepted. Even after on the Trail, they needed to ask directions. Grass growing in the road was evidence of low use. There were few gasoline stations, so a supply of fuel was carried along.

Until the early 1920s, travel to the park was usually by train (Tainter). But, as motor transportation became more reliable, it became preferable. Marc had previously gone by train, but being an adventurous lad, in 1924 decided to drive his 1914 "Royal Mail" Chevrolet roadster from Homer to the park. A day after he left he called to tell me that the engine bearings had all failed and asked if I could come out and salvage the battery and any other parts I wanted and then junk the car. He had rented a car storage space in a garage in a small village west of the Twin Cities for 30 days and then continued his journey to the park by train. A day before the rental was to expire, I and my brother Lyle drove my "490" Chevrolet touring car there. I took a complete set of connecting rod and main bearing shells with me and replaced all of the ruined ones in the car. Most automobile engines at that time had cast-in-place bearings but Chevrolet was unique in that bearings could be easily replaced. I drove that car to Homer while my brother Lyle followed in my car. After that year fisheries workers usually drove a large truck to the park and also carried equipment and supplies that would be needed that season.

The Trail crossed North Dakota. None of the roads were paved and were in especially poor condition because of the gumbo mud. This mud was very sticky and would roll up into balls or clods and accumulate under the fenders. Eventually so much would accumulate as to stop the truck. To clean out the mud, they carried short-handled shovels, but often bare hands worked as well. Progress could be painfully slow. One day in western North Dakota, they traveled only 6 miles (Tainter).

In the fall of 1924, a Reo Speed Wagon was transferred from some other government agency to the Homer, Minnesota, station for use at Homer and in Yellowstone Park (Tanner). The truck was in good condition although it was several years old. It had four cylinders and the brakes were open (not enclosed in housings), which required adjustments each day if traveling on sand or volcanic ash roads.

In the spring of 1925, a question arose concerning what would be the best and most economical way to get the truck to Yellowstone. The first thought was to ship it to Gardiner, Montana, have a garage unload it and store it, and hold it until the crew arrived later. Then it was decided that Marc Tainter and Swamp (Cleon H.) Walker would drive it through. Mr. Culler (our supervisor) gave Walker and Tanner a list of material and supplies that were to be taken from stock at the Homer station for transfer to Yellowstone. When this was collected, we found that we had some extra room left on the truck. So, we took this under advisement, as Frank Tainter would say, and he came up with the idea of making a frame and enclosing the bed of the truck with canvas. He had an old passenger car that he was not using, and we could have a seat from it. So, that was mounted on the rear of the truck facing backward. Taking two extra passengers on the truck would save the government the cost of railroad transportation.

About the twentieth of May 1925, Marc Tainter, Cleon Walker, Les Bennett, and Roger P. "Bill" Tanner boarded the above rig bound for Yellowstone Park. This was before the time of courtesy cards for gasoline and oil, but we did have scrip in a book of coupons worth about ten cents each, and we travelers were on a $5.00 per diem (per day expense). This took care of us very well. Over and above meals and lodging, we often had enough for a 5-cent cigar and to go to the best movie in town without using our own funds.

Before we reached the central part of Minnesota, we were out of improved roads. They were just trails and were usually graded for only a few miles out of town. Some towns didn't even have graveled streets. But there were bridges where needed if they had not been washed out. We did come to a dry run where the bridge was gone. We could get into the run from the side we were on but had to go about five miles in it before we could get out. We were favored by the weather.

We ran into a little trouble on a steep hill in western Dakota. Marc had the old truck in low gear but finally it could not make it any farther and the motor died. The truck started to drift backwards with him and neither the emergency nor foot brake would hold. Lucky for him he cut the rear end into the bank and stopped. He started forward again and two of us followed and when the motor was about dead we would scotch the wheels with rocks.

At another time on this trip, as we were gaining altitude, the motor would boil and we were getting low on radiator water. But we came to a ranch house and I went in for some. The lady of the house told me that her husband and their neighbor had gone for some that was hauled in by wagon and team. They had left before dawn and would not be back until after dark. She had some water on hand but requested that if there was any left after filling the radiator, I was to bring it back. The two families were homesteaders and neighbors. The water on that section of the country was "gyp" and could not be used.

We arrived in Gardiner, Montana, in about five days and went from there to the hatchery at Yellowstone Lake the next day. For early travelers coming from the East, the most convenient entrance into the park was at Gardiner. The east entrance through Sylvan Pass opened much later. The return trip at the end of the season in September was made from Yellowstone to Homer, Minnesota from the east entrance, designated as the southern route.

The trip in 1925 was Marc's last. That autumn he incurred a small cut on one of his fingers. Within a few days a blood infection had spread to his hand and rapidly proceeded up his arm to his shoulder. He suffered much pain and soon died. Penicillin had not yet been developed and little was known of the control of blood infections (Mary Adella Tainter). Marc's mother, the author's grandmother, told this author that experience when he was only 6 years old. Marc had enlisted in the army in 1918 and when he was in training at Fort Riley, Kansas, he, and hundreds of other recruits became infected with the 1918 influenza virus. He did survive *but his family later wondered if that virus infection had made him more susceptible to the blood infection that later took his life.*

Reo truck and crew (1925), ready to leave the Homer station. Left to right: Marc Tainter, Cleon Walker, Lester Bennett, and Bill Tanner. Tanner collection.

A hand-written verse by C. F. Culler on the back of this photo suggests the camaraderie of the personnel at the Homer station and his sense of leadership; "Their faults we write upon the sands, their virtues upon the tablets of love and memory. C.F.C."

In 1926, we used the same truck (Tanner). The crew consisted of Cleon Walker, Hugh Tainter, Gilmer Fuestel and Bill Tanner. There were some improvements on the highways. More of them had been graded and there was gravel on them. However, there remained a lot to be done, and there were many miles of just trails. There were no highway numbers or signs other than A, Y, or P.

We met a herd of sheep and their tenders and dogs in a small narrow canyon. We had to stop and after a while a tender came along and told us it would take a long time for the sheep to pass through. We asked how many sheep there might be. His reply was, "A good many." We asked if there might be a thousand.

His reply — "Many more." Then we asked if eight thousand would cover them.

His reply – "Maybe." They were on their way to pasture.

Sheep herd seen on way to Yellowstone National Park, 1927. Tainter collection.

Finally, we could be on our way. Farther down the road we stopped to answer nature's call. As soon as the truck stopped, I saw that it was sinking with all four wheels, and shouted to Tainter to give her the gun, but it was too late, and the wheels were soon down to the axles. There we were, miles from anywhere and we were helpless. After a while, we heard a motor running in the far distance; and in due time, here came a first World War army tank that had been transferred to the state for highway work. We had a good heavy chain and had it fast to the truck bumper by the time it reached us. We hitched on to the tank and were soon on our way.

The following day, we came to a newly graded road. It had been raining and it was necessary to hold the truck in the center of the road because it was slick as owl grease, and we could easily slide off into the ditch. We managed to keep control for miles, but finally we were meeting a motorcycle with a sidecar. Again Mr. Tainter was driving, and why not? That was his official job, and without a doubt he was the best driver of the bunch of us. He eased the truck over as much as he thought he dared but about that time he noticed that the operator of the motorcycle was a lady. The gentleman that he was, he figured that he could give her just a little more of the road, but it was too late. Our truck headed for the ditch and the lady passed on in the center of the road.

With one wheel in the ditch, we went on as far as we could but finally came to a culvert and had to stop. There was nothing to do but wait, and WAIT we did!

Finally, luck was with us again as two four-wheel-drive army trucks pulled up back of us. These trucks were transferred from the army to state highways. The driver of the lead truck noted that we were set up to be pulled out of the ditch, so he instructed us to hitch on to his truck and he would have us out and back on the road in five minutes. This attempt failed. We were up to the culvert by this time and the rear state truck had to hitch on to our truck and pull it back down the road. The driver of the front state truck said, "Well, there is nothing we can do for you. We will have to leave you here."

Then Hugh Tainter had an idea that he thought might work and asked the state drivers if they would give us another try. The idea was to hitch one truck to the front and the other to the back of our truck- - the back truck to be in reverse and the front truck in forward gear. Believe it or not, the trick worked. Our truck was back on the road and we were soon on our way. The state drivers did not have to get out of their trucks, but we were muddy from head to foot.

A few hours later, we arrived at a very nice little town. We put the truck in storage for the night, washed the mud off the lower part of our boots and proceeded on to the hotel where we fully expected to be turned down for lodging but were not. When we finished registering, the clerk told us that there was a washroom and laundry in the basement that we were welcome to use. We took advantage of this offer by washing our hip boots and putting our blue denim jackets and overalls through the washer.

From there into Gardiner traveling was as good as could be expected, and we made the trip in 5 ½ days. I don't recall any delays or mishaps on our return from Yellowstone to Homer in September. So far each of the two falls had been very dry and a bit of moisture would have been welcome.

In 1927, the crew consisted of Hugh Tainter, Cleon Walker, Bill Tanner, and I believe, Harry Heuver. The trip was made, as usual, by truck and earlier than usual; I believe about the tenth of May. Everything went wrong on this trip. In some parts, the frost was hardly out of the ground. We were stuck a few times before we were out of Minnesota, and it seemed to get worse as we moved westward.

We came to one place where the small bridge had been washed out. The opening was not over three feet wide and perhaps 1 ½-feet deep and was full of water. We hit it with the front wheels and were going fast enough to bounce them out, but the driver's idea was to stop, which we did, with back wheels in the depression. There we were! What were we going to do? There had not been another vehicle over that trail that spring. There were no logs, rocks, or brush around there to put in the hole. But, we had a railroad jack along with us, so Tainter came up with another idea. That was to take the staples out of the fence posts along the road, pull the posts, put them under the wheels and drive out, then gather up the posts out of the water, put them back in their holes and replace the staples. It worked!

After this, we were really wet and muddy. After registering in at the best hotel in Livingston, Montana, you can be assured the hotel clerk sent us to their basement to get cleaned up before going to our rooms. On our ninth day out from Homer, we arrived in Gardiner, Montana, where we were to have picked up part of the crew going to the Lake Hatchery. They had come in by train and our supervisor, Mr. C. F. Culler, was one of the fellows waiting for us. He wanted to know why we did not let him know what our delay was. In that area back in those days, long distance phone service was unheard of; but we could send all the government-rate telegrams that were necessary for $.25 each. Our only instruction from Mr. Culler had been that we would meet in Gardiner. The crew arrived June 5 after a considerable delay enroute [4].

Stranded on the road, pulling fence posts to fill a hole in the bridge, 1927. Drawing by Roxanne Chase.

For the first crew into the park, the difficulties encountered on the road to the park often continued once in the park. When J. H. Brunson was dispatched to reopen the Soda Butte facility on June 9, 1918 [5], he reached Gardiner without incident the following day. He was then intercepted by a flood that carried away the bridge over the Lamar River. He had to wait a week before a temporary bridge could be contrived. Although 600,000 eggs were taken at Soda Butte, the lack of transportation facilities made it impossible to ship green eggs to Bozeman. Extremely hot weather had melted heavy snow deposits in the park and surrounding watersheds and many bridges and roads were washed out. The railroad from Livingston to Gardiner was also out for some time that season.

In 1927, the crew's troubles were only just beginning. For 10 miles between Canyon Junction and the lake, several washouts from heavy snowfall made the road almost impassable [6]. *The information Mr. Culler had from the Yellowstone Park rangers was that no roads in the park had yet been opened, that most of them were covered with heavy snow, but that they would furnish us with two four-wheel drive trucks and drivers to help us get to the Lake hatchery (Tanner).*

The next morning, we started out bright and early from the park headquarters at Mammoth. We had gone only a few miles up into the mountains when the two park trucks were stopped and chained together. We were ordered to chain our truck onto theirs. We already had a Dodge roadster tied to our truck. A ranger was taking it through to the ranger station. So, there we went with all four vehicles tied together. It was good that we had canned beans and corned beef along or somebody would have gone hungry. The trucks did not follow the roads by a long shot, and it was a wonder that they got through.

Late in the afternoon, we reached the Canyon Ranger Station and were told that our troubles were just beginning. There was a washout on the road leading to the lake. All the work needed to repair the road back in those days was done by horse teams, wagons, slipscrapers, etc. But there was nothing of this kind there, and it would be necessary for us hatchery men to make repairs with pick and shovel and a few wheelbarrows we could borrow from the ranger station.

The Canyon Rangers put us up for the night, and they treated us to one of the most delicious dinners I ever had. Of course, we were all hungry which made the food better. There were not enough bunks to take of all of us fellows, but the rangers had a lot of blankets that helped a lot on the hard floors. The rangers also gave us breakfast the next morning

The second morning out of Canyon we were on the job to fill in the washout so we could get on to the hatchery. It was really some hole to tackle with hand tools. The work went rather fast because the ground was mostly sand and volcanic ash and there was no stone or frost in the ground. About 1 p. m., Mr. Culler asked Frank Tainter and me if we would walk on to the hatchery and bring the Model T Ford back to the washout the next morning so he, the lady cook and her husband could get transportation out to the hatchery. Mr. Tainter was getting along in years and this was a long hike for him, but we reached the Ranger Station at the lake about an hour before sunset.

Harry Leake, the ranger in charge, asked us to have supper with them. Mr. Tainter and I went on to the hatchery, made a fire in the bunkhouse, checked the hatchery and mess house to see if the bears had done any damage, then back to the ranger station for supper, then to our own bunkhouse and bed. Mr. Tainter said that was the longest walk he had ever taken in his life. We were soon in bed and fast asleep.

We were up the next morning at the crack of dawn, pumped up the tires on the Model T with a hand pump, filled the gas tank, stopped at the ranger station for breakfast, and were at the washout by the time the other men got there. I went back to my shovel job, Mr. Tainter transported our supervisor, the lady chef and her husband to the hatchery, and came back for some groceries and supplies we had brought with us from Homer.

I went back to the Canyon Ranger Station with the rest of the crew for the night and slept on the floor. We had the repairs to the road made in three days so we could get the truck across. We had purchased food in Gardiner, and it was good that we did as it was almost three days before the roads were considered to be passable back to Gardiner.

This had been a long hard trip. We were usually on the road soon after daylight and were there until near dark. We were lucky that we did not have to spend a night or two on the truck.

The lake in 1927 was much higher than normal and the work of constructing racks in the creeks where egg collections were made was not completed until June 10 [7].

In 1928, we left Homer the latter part of May with a brand new 1 1/2 – ton truck – a Graham Dodge truck. The canopy and back seat had been removed from the old Reo Speed Wagon and placed on this truck. The crew was Hugh Tainter, Cleon Walker, Harry Heuver, and Roger Tanner. This was the best trip we had to Yellowstone, not much trouble or delays until we were along the Yellowstone River somewhere near Billings, when we came to a hot springs hotel and resort. There was a rope stretched across the road with a sign, "Road closed, stop and inquire." By that time, someone from the hotel came out and told us that there was about to be a slide on the road up along the mountain. At that time, it was moving a little and it was not safe to go on. We inquired about going around but were advised that would be about 200 miles out of our way. The advice to us was that *the state highway commission had men at each end of the slide and they were watching for movement. When the sun went down, the move would be stopped by freezing or colder weather at the point; and by four o'clock the next morning it would be safe to pass over. We stayed at the hotel for a nice dinner and good bed, and at four o'clock the next morning the manager called us and told us to get dressed and leave at once, that he would have coffee ready in fruit jars when we came downstairs. We started right away, and believe me it was cold riding on that back seat.*

Not far up the road we came to a flagman who advised us to put the truck in low gear and to take it very easy, as too much of a jar might start the slide moving again. We obeyed orders and went on our way. This slide did break loose that afternoon and it took the state more than a year to get that part of the road open again. Our return to Homer in September was, as usual, very good.

(Above) Railroad passenger depot at Gardiner, 1927. Tainter collection.

(Right) North entrance at Gardiner, 1927. Tainter collection.

Fish Culture in Yellowstone National Park

(Upper left and right) Breaking the road to Lake. Tainter collection.

(Lower) Harry Heuver (left) and Hugh Tainter helping with road opening in 1927.

H. Tainter said of the experience, "Our feet were soaking wet and nearly frozen from standing in the slushy ice. We were perspiring profusely from the exertion of shoveling snow, and mosquitoes were eating us alive." Tainter collection.

Frank Tainter seated on top of truck cab, June 1, 1928.
Saeugling collection.

South entrance, coming from Jackson Hole, Wyoming, 1927.
Tainter collection.

East entrance, 1927. Tainter collection.

Getting ready to leave the park in the fall, before the snow got too deep, 1927. Tainter collection.

Frank H. Tainter Ph.D.

*National Park Service road grader plowing snow, 1927.
Tainter collection.*

THE RANGERS

The cooperation between the park rangers and the fisheries personnel was perfect, and any request from one to the other was fulfilled (Tanner). I remember one afternoon when my good friend, Harry Leak, came to me at the hatchery and said, "Bill, there is a fire across the lake, and I want you to take me over there. My reply was that we would have to have permission from my foreman, Harry Heuver, to use the boat. There was a terrible storm on the lake when we contacted Mr. Heuver. His reply was no, he would not send any man out in that storm. The ranger said that he was deputizing me and that he had the power to do so. After an argument between the two, our foreman gave in, turned to me and said, "Bill. This is not an order; but if you feel that you can make the trip safely, you may go ahead."

Soon my running mate, the Robinson lad, the ranger and I were on one of our 35 ft. cruisers and on our way. Soon the ranger became sick, unloaded his dinner and lay down. The storm was really bad, and our progress was slow. When darkness came, we were still out on the lake and bouncing. We could see the fire and the ranger said it was a dead pine tree and had been struck by lightning. Soon the moon was up. We had a supper of canned beans, corned beef and coffee.

By this time, we were nearing the south arm of the lake that was becoming quiet. And finally, we reached a point in the lake where conditions were perfect for landing. The fire was in view. I eased the bow of the boat on shore, and the ranger and my helper eased themselves off the boat, each with a pick and shovel.

I then backed the boat out a safe distance in the lake, dropped the anchor, went into the engine room, turned the collar of my big sheepskin coat up around my head, lay down along the warm engine, and was soon *fast asleep. The following morning the sun was well up when I awoke. Soon the two men returned from fighting the fire and said everything was under control. They had cut down the tree and buried it in the volcanic ash, making sure there were no live coals to start another fire. They came aboard and soon we were on our way back to the hatchery. Again, we had a meal of coffee, canned beans, and corned beef.*

One other duty of our ranger naturalist at the lake was guiding tours and lecturing about the points of interest there. He would begin at the tourist camp, go to the hotel and then to the hatchery, — people joining in as he went along. Often there would be 50 or more in the group. This was a walking tour of about a half-mile long. His lectures were about birds, flowers, woods life, or any other subject the tourists wanted to discuss.

When they reached the hatchery, he would take the group back of the building where a small stream came from the woods and ran into the lake. At spawning time, a small fish trap was set up in this stream; and there would be some fish in it to be spawned. By this time, one of the hatchery men would be on the job to show the group just how the operations were carried on. Since their arrival, he had been telling the tourists about the number of streams we worked, approximate number of eggs taken yearly, and the number of employees required for the three-month season, etc.

After seeing egg-taking, the group moved on through the hatchery room and were shown how the eggs were handled. The hatchery employee explained that they could be safely handled for the first 24 hours. After that time, they were in the tender stage and should not be handled until they became eyed. Then, until about hatching time, they were taken off the trays and put into a tub of water and shocked by stirring them around by hand. Then they were put back on the trays and the dead or infertile eggs were removed. After this was done, they were ready for shipment or setting up for hatching. Then the tourists went happily on their way.

During my second season in Yellowstone Park, I took care of the aquarium as I did in La Crosse, along with showing groups of park visitors making their first daily stop at the first hatchery and aquarium how trout eggs were taken and fertilized (Saeugling). Dr. Kelly, Professor at Cornell College,

Mt. Vernon, Iowa, guided groups. I recall on one occasion he had about 40 tourists. After stripping the eggs from a nice female and fertilizing the eggs with sperm from a male trout and explaining all the details, the group departed. One middle-aged sweetheart remained, came forward and stating that she could not see what took place standing in back of the others and asked if I would do it again. I told her, "Yes, very kindly." When fertilizing the eggs, she asked if it didn't hurt the trout. I said, "No ma'am. They love it." With a twinkle in her eye and a smile on her face, she walked away. I can still see that beautiful face and expression.

Of all the men coming and going in our work, I know of only two who finally had hard feelings toward each other. They were Eliga Gear and Archie Capell. They were both past 50 years old when they came to Yellowstone. They became very good friends and were assigned to hatchery work — taking care of the eggs, packing them for shipment, and handling the newly-hatched fry and small fingerlings. Their bunk beds were beside each other, they sat by each other for their meals, and wherever they went they were together. In 1926, they decided that they would like to go to Clear Creek the next season for taking eggs there. So, in 1927 they were assigned to Clear Creek with a helper. They were not much more than set up for work when Mr. Gear told Mr. Capell that he would be in charge of it. Mr. Capell said, "No. I have more years of service with the Government, and this is my job." The disagreement was about whom was to write-up the daily log on operations and sign it. I think this was settled by alternating the write-up and signing them. Their work was perfect, and they returned to the Lake hatchery soon after spawn-taking was over.

But they were not the same toward each other. Their bunks were clear across the room from each other, and they did not sit together at the table. Very soon Mr. Capell requested that he be sent home and did not ask to come back in 1928 (Tanner).

Frank H. Tainter Ph.D.

HERBERT HOOVER, SECRETARY OF COMMERCE

James Banner, Carey Bunch and I were at Peale Island when we were told that Mr. Herbert Hoover, Secretary of Commerce, would be in Yellowstone Park soon and would probably come to see us (Tanner). We were thrilled, as could be expected, but did not make any special effort to get ready for his visit. We finally heard that he was stopping at the Lake Hotel and would be over soon.

Roy Ripley was a well-qualified boatman on Lake Michigan, from the Charlevoix hatchery, and was brought into Yellowstone each season to operate one of the boats to pick up the eggs from Peale Island and Clear Creek egg-taking stations, and to take them to the hatchery for incubation. He was a good cook; and if we were not back to the cabin in time, he would make dinner for himself and the lad who was with our crew.

On this special day, Roy came into the creek where we were taking eggs and landed the boat. Mr. Hoover swung himself off and came over to where we were working and said, "Boys, I am Herbert Hoover. Don't let me interfere with your work." He watched us for a while and then went back to the boat. Roy picked up a few fish for dinner and then went on to our cabin to cook for all of us.

We finished our egg-taking for the day and loaded our take into our small boat. By the time we reached the dock at our cabin, Mr. Hoover was there to meet us.

He had convinced our supervisor, Mr. Culler, that he wanted that day to be alone with us field men and to see how operations were carried on. Soon after we started to eat, he told us that this was one of the most enjoyable days he had spent since he started to work for the United States government as a civil engineer; and he would appreciate it if we would forget who he was and call him by his first name, or Mr. Hoover if desired, but to please forget his title for the day. For the rest of the day, he was Mr. Hoover to us.

He told us about being sent to Florida to build the first levee around Lake Okeechobee after the great flood at about the turn of the century that drowned so many people. This was before the time of big equipment with which to do that work. There is some of the old levee left that is about 4 to 5 ft. high. A new levee has been constructed which is 30 ft. or more in height. At that time, little did I think I would ever fish in that lake; but I do. When Mr. Hoover built the first levee, it was done by mule power and two-wheel scrapers, with black men to drive the teams.

When Mr. Hoover was leaving, he told us how much he had enjoyed the day. He noticed that we had a few extra bunks and asked if we would put him up if he could get away. Our reply, "Yes." He then informed us that he would have to look over his itinerary; and if it was not too crowded, he would be back. He thought he would like to try cooking again and have a workout on our woodpile. On his way from our cabin to the boat, he stopped at our woodpile, picked up the axe and swung it at a block of wood. It popped open. He looked at it and said, "I am slipping. I was off center a bit but that's not bad since I have been away from an axe for twenty-five years."

We loaded the eggs onto Mr. Ripley's boat, and they were on their way to Clear Creek and the hatchery. We enjoyed Mr. Hoover and were sorry he did not have more time to spend with us.

Frank H. Tainter Ph.D.

CALVIN COOLIDGE, PRESIDENT OF THE UNITED STATES

In 1927, President Coolidge was in the Black Hills of South Dakota for his summer vacation and came into Yellowstone Park for a brief time (Tanner). Since it was the duty and pleasure of the employees at the hatchery to do whatever we could for the enjoyment of the president while he was there, arrangements were made to give him a fishing trip on Lake Yellowstone one afternoon.

When the day came for this trip, our two best boats were spic and span and ready. At noon, Mr. Culler told us that the President and his party would be at the hatchery at 1 p. m. He would introduce us to the President, and it was usually customary to shake hands with him. When he arrived, we were ready for the introduction. Mr. Culler called one name, and the President held up his hand. He announced that he would be unable to shake hands with the crew as he had been doing a lot of that, and his hand was almost paralyzed. Then he nodded as the names were called. When this was finished, the crew went on to their work; and we who were going fishing on to the boats.

Mr. Culler and Cleon Walker manned the boat for the President and two Secret Service men; and Hugh Tainter and I had the second boat with four Secret Service men aboard. The spot we had selected for fishing was not far from the hatchery, and we were soon there.

It was a perfect day to be on the lake. The water was clear, about ten feet deep; and we could see plenty of fish around the boat. The other boat was anchored fairly close to us, and we could see what was going on over there. The President and Mr. Culler were fishing hard but not catching any. Soon after anchoring, I had rigged up my rod, but was waiting for someone else to get going. So, I turned to the Secret Service men and asked them why they were not ready. One replied. "Mr. Tanner, you wouldn't think of taking a fish before the President, would you?" I had not thought of it that way.

Finally, through coaching from Mr. Culler and Walker, the President slowed down enough for a fish to catch the lure as he was pulling it in. That was the signal for us to go to work. The catch limit at that time was 10 fish and the President was the only one to catch that many. We returned to the hatchery, and the President had a very enjoyable afternoon.

We had many distinguished guests to take on boat trips: Congressmen, Senators, and other government people, and their friends. I had made quite a few trips with Roy Ripley; and he told the boss that I was capable of handling the boats and, if he was not available, to send me out. On a few trips, I took our park naturalist, a professor from Cedar Rapids, Iowa, and his party. I do not remember his name. His favorite places were in the vicinity of Columbine Creek to view the beautiful flowers, then on to Pelican and Gull Islands to see the eggs of young birds there.

A view of the porch of the mess house at the Lake Hatchery, 1927. The young people are employees of the Lake Hotel or various camps located in the vicinity. Tainter collection.

Capt. C. F. Culler in 1928. Elsie Morris, his stenographer, is on his right. Mrs. Frank (Mary Adella) Tainter is on his left. Tainter collection.

Calvin Coolidge visits the park and hatchery operations, 1927. Tainter collection.

Fish Culture in Yellowstone National Park

C. F. Culler entering the fishing boat, 1927. Cleon Walker is holding the boat, and Calvin Coolidge is waiting to enter the boat. Tainter collection.

Cleon Walker, C. F. Culler, and Calvin Coolidge, fishing in Lake Yellowstone, 1927. Tainter collection.

Frank H. Tainter Ph.D.

THE WONDER OF IT ALL

"Where the West begins
Out where the handclasp's a little stronger, Out where the smile dwells a little longer, That's where the West begins.
Where there's more of singing and less of sighing, Where there's more of giving and less of buying, And a man makes friends without half trying, That's where the West begins." *

* Poem printed on cover of souvenir photograph album purchased in Yellowstone Park in 1927 by Hugh F. Tainter.

To the seasonal employees and young men who were culturists in Yellowstone, the park was a wondrous place, indeed. There was little time allowed, however, to enjoy the scenic and natural wonders. Once started, the fish collection and spawning operation went along as necessary and any enjoyment had to be gotten from the immediate vicinity.

In those days, time did not mean anything to us (Tanner). We were paid by the month; and if there was a job to be done, the sooner it was finished, the sooner we would get out of there. We worked 16 hours on some days and always worked 7 days a week. We did not know about or expect overtime pay. At our home stations, however, we worked 40 hours per week. During the tour of duty in the park, there were only two days off; the Fourth of July and one Sunday for a truck trip around the park. On the Fourth, we were up bright and early and went to the mess hall at the Lake Hatchery for breakfast. There we visited with our old friends, met others who had come in after we had left the hatchery earlier in the season, had lunch and supper with them, and returned to Clear Creek, all in the same day.

The free day would include a sight-seeing trip around part of the park. Although a side trip north to the Grand Canyon of the Yellowstone River might have been done some years, the main part of the day was spent touring the geysers at West Thumb, the Upper and Lower Geyser Basins, and perhaps the Norris Geyser Basin as well.

In those days, handkerchief pool was popular (Tainter). You would throw your dirty hankie in the pool. The current of boiling hot water would carry it down and around and several minutes later it would come out all clean. One day when I was there, it was clogged and would not circulate and wash the handkerchiefs. I took a piece of telephone wire, bent a hook on the end and, after fishing around awhile, came up with over one-hundred hankies. I kept them and did not have to buy any new hankies for years. Later, I understand, vandals threw rocks into the pool and it became plugged up.

Terrace at Mammoth Hot Springs, 1927. Tainter collection.

The Hoo Doos, 1927. Tainter collection.

(Right) The Golden Gate, 1927. Tainter collection.

(Below) Swan Lake Flat, 1927. Tainter collection.

Lake Sylvan, 1927. Tainter collection.

Sylvan Pass, 1927. Tainter collection.

Fish Culture in Yellowstone National Park

Crossover loop in road to east entrance. Tainter collection.

The Firehole River, 1927. Tainter collection.

(Above) Chittenden Bridge, 1927. Tainter collection.

(Right) Hugh Tainter and Bill Tanner at Handkerchief Pool, 1927. Tainter collection.

Mammoth Paint Pots at Thumb, 1927. Tainter collection.

Teakettle Spring, with Old Faithful Inn in background, 1927. Tainter collection.

Inn at Old Faithful, with 1925 Dodge fish hatchery truck in foreground, 1927. Tainter collection.

Yellowstone Park Transportation Co. vehicle, with accommodations for driver and eleven passengers. Top and curtains could be put up in case of rain. Tanner collection.

(Above) The Model T Ford runabout, 1928. Margaret Tainter, sister of Hugh and Marc, is seated in back. Tainter collection.

(Right) Cleon "Swamp" Walker, horsing around on the Model T Ford runabout, 1927. Walker was on detail to the Homer station from Louisiana, hence, the nickname, "Swamp".
Tainter collection.

The personnel had two days off during the season, July 4 and a Sunday for a trip around the park, 1925 or 1926. Cleon Walker sitting above spare tire, next to him is a seasonal lad named Galigher. In second row, center man is Clyde Adams, next to him with tie and facing camera is Bill Tanner. Tanner collection.

Part of the fisheries crew, on park day, about to depart on a day of sightseeing, probably in 1929. Standing: Hugh Tainter; in cab, Jack Bunch; on truck from left to right, unknown, Ed Barker, Ted Feustal, Eldon Saeugling, John Garner, Harry Heuver, Harry Carson, Fielding Tanner, Jimmy Banner, George Eisenlohr, Ed Johnson, Dick Fenucan. Tainter collection.

Hatchery personnel and female employees of the nearby camps or hotel, getting ready for campout on shore of Lake Yellowstone, 1925 or 1926. From left: (3) Edward Hill, seasonal employee and student from Ames, Iowa, (5) Bill Tanner, and (9) Cleon Walker. Tanner collection.

Frank H. Tainter Ph.D.

BEAR ME IN MIND

The native black or brown bears and grizzly bears periodically caused much damage to the spawn collection facilities [1]. The first year the bears caused much trouble was in 1915 [2]. This followed a very severe winter and hungry bears leaving hibernation raided fish traps. So much damage occurred that the traps were removed.

In 1917, bears caused much annoyance on the east side of the lake[3]. The winter of 1916-17 had excessive snow and the season began about 10 days late.

Even though significant damage did not always result, activities of the bears were a source of constant amusement and often consternation to the hatchery employees.

In 1925, while four of us were at the Clear Creek station, we occasionally noticed a yearling bear near our living quarters (Tanner). We went to work one day and evidently failed to close the front door. When we came back to the house (an old frame building), one of the screens was knocked out of a window and a bag of flour that we had left on the table by the stove was missing. Then we saw a line of flour on the ground leading into the woods. I followed this; and when I had gone about two hundred yards, I came to the end of the flour. Just a little farther on was the empty sack. Evidently, the bear had snagged it when he went out of the window. We never saw him or any other bears around there again.

One summer after egg-taking was over, Cleon Walker, Roy Ripley, Mr. Wagner, three other men and I were sent over to the southeast arm of the lake, where the Yellowstone River comes into it, to put in a fish trap. Trials had been made for this purpose before; but due to high water, they never held. It was thought that if we went farther upstream one might hold. We had a tent to set up for night housing and our first day was used in getting it ready for housekeeping. We placed long grass on the bottom, pine boughs on top of this, and three or four blankets for a mattress. We had other blankets for cover. The second day after setting up camp we started to get logs for the foundation of the trap.

A few nights later, Mr. Wagner decided we should have some candy, so he made a nice batch that we all enjoyed. We cleaned up the mess and soon afterwards were asleep. All at once someone began to shout that there was a bear in the tent! We turned our flashlights on and Mr. Bear left - - We had not tied the door shut on our tent, so we did so, thinking that would keep Mr. Bear out, and again we were fast asleep. The first thing we knew someone was shouting that the bear was tearing into the tent. We soon had our flashlights lighted again. Mr. Bear had torn a big hole in the side of our tent, had taken the dishrag that we had used to wash up after making candy and he was happily on his way. He did not give us any more trouble that night or thereafter.

The above work was finished in about a week or ten days, and we returned to the Lake Hatchery. The following spring when this point was checked for putting in a fish trap there was no sign of the foundation we had made. Everything had been washed away.

It was necessary for the boats to be cleaned before they were launched into the lake to be used in the spawn taking and other operations. Well, I was doing just this early one spring in 1927 after we came to the park. The boat was stored alongside the hatchery building. I was enjoying the nice warm sun and my work when I suddenly heard bear talk coming down from the woods. When I looked around, I saw a very large mother bear and three cubs ambling very slowly along. She was telling the babies that she was taking them down to the lake for their first bath, how much fun it would be, and how much they would enjoy it.

By this time mother and cubs were at the water's edge. The mother sat down on the bank just out of the water and continued her instructions. There was one cub much smaller than the other two. This little one did not appear to be much interested in his mother's instructions, and less interested in a bath. After a while the mother moved about 10 feet into the lake where the water was about six inches deep, and she sat down. All this time she was instructing and coaxing the babies to come to her. The two larger ones advanced a few steps but thought the water was too cold, and they started back to shore. The mother continued coaxing and soon the two large ones started in again. When the water reached their tummies, they stopped and put in a high arch in their backs to take their tummies out of that cold stuff. The mother kept coaxing and soon the cubs went to her. All this time she was telling them to go ahead and have a good time in the water. Soon they were splashing and ducking each other, and they were really enjoying this new adventure.

While the mother was working with the two larger cubs, you could see that the runt was not the least bit interested in getting into that cold water. Now she began to work with it, and he would make an effort by taking a few steps in the water but would turn and run back to shore. So, the mother came back out on the bank and gave him a good talking to—She then returned to the water and sat down and started coaxing again. The bear then came part way to her but then decided he was going to get out of there. The mother let out a rough demand and the little fellow stopped, went to her and crawled up on her lap. The mother was telling him there was no danger and he was to get in the water and have a good time. But he didn't like the idea and would rather go ashore. At this time, the mother drew her baby to her body and gave him a few swats on the bottom; and he was glad to get into the water. He ventured over a little bit closer to the other two cubs and they gave him a couple of duckings, so he beat it back to mom and she soon let him get out on the bank. This lasted about a half hour. The two larger cubs thought this was a wonderful experience, but the baby would just as soon be a landlubber.

Soon after the above episode, I was one of three men sent to Peale Island to take eggs from the two streams nearby and did not return to the Lake Hatchery for about six weeks.

When we arrived back at the Lake Hatchery after finishing the Peale Island work, about the first person I met was the camp boy about 12 to 14 years old. He was from Winona, Minnesota; and we had met before.

Right away he began telling me about the mother bear and three cubs who spent a good share of their time near the hatchery and were at the garbage dump both morning and evening when he took the garbage up. He asked me to go along with him that evening, which I did; it was the mother and her cubs that I had seen at the lake for the cubs' first bath. The babies had grown quite a bit, but still the runt was much smaller than the other two.

The mother bear was very gentle, but yet she wanted the public to keep their distance from her and her babies. She usually stayed near the hatchery and road. People would often stop and toss them food. One early morning I was back in the woods for something; and on my way back, I saw a young mother with her little boy, about four years old.

She was coaxing him to walk down to the mother bear for a picture. I happened to see them at this time and noticed that the child was between the mother bear and the cubs. I was close enough to talk to the lady without raising my voice and told her not to say a word or move. She followed my instructions. Mother bear moved down to the child and stood there for a few seconds by his side, talking to him in bear language; and then went on over to her babies. Again, I told the lady not to move. By this time, the mother bear was a little farther away and I walked to the child and led him to his mother.

Another close call—I was on the road with a truck. I saw three men and a small boy get out of their car to feed a yearling bear alongside the road. I gave a short blast on the horn, but the people did not hear it. The little boy walked over to the bear and held his hand up high. The bear stood up expecting to find some food, but there was none. When it started down, it stopped at the boy's midsection and left four nasty tusk marks across the boy's stomach. By this time, I was up to them. The father showed me the marks on the boy and his remarks were that the bear should be killed. The bear was still standing by the road expecting a handout.

Time was marching on and the entire hatchery crew had fallen in love with the bear family in and around our garbage dump. The camp boy had been well instructed about how to conduct himself around this family and had made good friends with them. He would tell you that he understood bear's language perfectly; and when she told him to move on, he moved.

By this time mother bear had taught her babies to hang out down by the road and to go to the tourist's cars when they stopped, and climb up on the running boards, and accept food when it was offered to them. This was very cute and enjoyable for the tourists. Mother bear never went any closer than the bank of the road but kept a sharp eye out to see that her babies were treated right. As time went on, the cubs became bolder and found that if they were on the road the cars would be more likely to stop. They soon learned not to try to flag a yellow bus because they would not stop, and never had food to share. This was fairly true with trucks but there were times when they would take chances.

One afternoon the boy who was working with me (I don't remember his name or where he was from) and I took a load of fingerling trout and stocked streams in the vicinity of Thumb Ranger Station and were returning to the hatchery. There was a park truck ahead of us. We were very near the hatchery when the truck came to a sudden stop. About this time, I saw the mother bear on the road bank. The driver of the park road truck jumped out, picked up one of the cubs and threw it in the back of the truck. By that time, we were up to him and I was out of our truck. I asked him if he had run over the cub and his answer was, "Yes." Then I asked if he was going to report it to the rangers. His answer was, "Blankety blank bears are a nuisance." That evening I made it a point to ask my good friend Harry Leak who was in charge of the Lake Ranger Station if the truck driver had reported the kill. He said he did and had turned in the dead cub.

When I returned to the hatchery from the Ranger Station, the camp boy was waiting for me and wanted me to go to our garbage dump with him. I could see that he was worried and I suspected that he had missed the cub. As soon as we got away from the other men, he began to tell that when he took the garbage up a short time before only the mother and two larger cubs were there for their supper and that the mother was very much disturbed and worried, and that she tried to tell him something, but he could not understand what she wanted. When we reached the garbage dump, the bears were gone. As we headed back to the hatchery, we passed some large pine trees. The lad mentioned that sometimes the mother bear would put the cubs up in those trees and leave them there if she was going to be away for awhile. About that time, he discovered the cubs in separate trees and again began to wonder about the third cub. At this point, I had to tell him what had happened to it that afternoon. He came over to me, put his head on my chest and cried like a baby. Perhaps I might have shed a few tears myself.

Now his question was, "Where is the mother?" I did the best I could with the answers and told the lad that perhaps she was out looking for the missing baby, and maybe she would be back by morning. But it was forty-eight hours before mother bear returned to her cubs and her food at her garbage dump. The lad had done well for the bears as he made regular deposits of our garbage and had tried to coax the cubs down from the trees for something to eat. He had talked the cook out of cans of condensed milk and put it in pans at the foot of the trees, but the cubs' mother had told them to stay up there until her return, and so they did.

Soon afterwards the lad returned to his home in Winona, Minnesota. We had planned that we would get together that fall after I returned to Homer but that did not happen. I have not been to Homer or to Yellowstone Park since that time in 1928.

ANOTHER BEAR STORY

One day I took some supplies and groceries to the crew working at the Soda Butte Station (Tainter). We had to carry everything to the cabin located behind Fish Lake which was located about ½ mile from the road. As it was rather late when we finished, the crew invited me to stay there that night; and I could leave early next day with eggs to take back to the Lake Hatchery. The groceries were left piled on the kitchen table.

That night after we had gone to bed and were fast asleep, I awoke to feel a bear rubbing against the side of my bunk. I was in the top bunk and by the moonlight could see several bears methodically going through each parcel and breaking it open if they could. They broke open the flour sack and scattered flour all over. I didn't hear a peep out of the other fellows, one in the bunk right under me. I somehow knew that they were wide awake. Finally, the bears left. After a decent interval, a flashlight came on and the fellows went down to the hatchery building, got a couple of boards, a hammer and nails, and nailed the boards over the inside of the door. They repeated that procedure every night for the rest of the time they were there. They also insisted that I sleep in the bottom bunk and they drew straws to see who would get the top bunk.

The author of the 1915 annual report of the Bozeman Station had these words about the bears [4]. *The interest in the Bureau's operations has, however, not been confined to the official Park circles. The Park bear early evinced a great curiosity in and hearty appreciation of the work of the Bureau, besides exhibiting a warmer interest in the person of the fish culturist than the latter thought warranted or met with his approval, when the latter was obliged to use his tent jointly as living room, dining room and kitchen, as well as storeroom.*

Likewise, when previous experience had taught him to use his last remaining ham as a pillow, in a vain endeavor to preserve it from his officious friends, then finally to lose both pillow and breakfast at one swoop, besides having his slumbers thus rudely disturbed, was not only somewhat of a shock to the nerves, but was decidedly distressing to the stomach of the fish culturist, however pleasant it may have been to that of Brother Bruin.

This same Brother Bruin also had a bad habit of prying around the open-air hatcheries by day, as well as by night. To be busily and intently engaged in picking eggs by lantern light, then suddenly experience that feeling that one's privacy had been invaded by unbidden guests, then to look up into the shining eyes of a huge and possibly hungry grizzly, was an experience enjoyable only in the after telling. When turning hastily towards camp, only to find the mate to the aforesaid huge and possibly hungry grizzly peering intently at you from out of the encircling gloom, the atmosphere becomes tense. A moment of suspense, then a quick, astonished "Wugh" followed by a hasty, lumbering departure from either direction permits your hat to again settle back on your head. Nerves, however, are in no condition to continue the interrupted work or even for slumber. The calm and poise of some of our women pickers has more than once been disturbed at midday by finding the inquisitive gaze of a big black or brown bear fastened attentively on them. Fortunately, the bear are well fed during the tourist season on the garbage from the hotels.

Only last year, a big black bear, attracted by the smell of provisions, leaped through the screened window of one of our east side camps and landed alongside the bed of the then solitary and sleeping occupant. We have always been unable to determine whether man or beast was the more frightened.

All bears are great fishermen. More than once we have found them fishing in our traps, sometimes arriving on the scene in time to see the burly begger sitting on his haunches beside our trap and finishing what appeared to be a most enjoyable meal on the fish we had unwittingly assisted him in catching.

Frank H. Tainter Ph.D.

MORE BEARS

During my fifth year in Yellowstone Park (1932), the bears were so destructive, robbing the fish traps of adult trout to feed their cubs with (Saeugling). No trout were left for spawning purposes. It was then necessary to use 2,000 ft. webbing Fyke nets in 10 to 20 ft. of water depth in the lake to catch spawning trout. After two years of operation and only a small percent of nice spawning trout captured by this method, it was discontinued along with collecting and hatching operations. The Lake Hatchery was closed after a decision to let the trout perform in their natural way. From a no limit on trout catch to 2 fish per day after all hatchery operations ceased seemed to alleviate the situation. When I visited the park 5 years later, the newer methods seemed to be working satisfactorily.

(Right) Mr. Dude, the bear, with one of the seasonal employees. Tanner collection.

(Below) The mother bear and her two surviving cubs referred to in the text, 1928. Tainter collection.

Hugh Tainter and Harry Heuver, the night they accidently drove the Model T into the dump at Lake and scared the bears. Drawing by Roxanne Chase.

Webbing Fyke nets used in early 1930s to catch spawning trout in Lake Yellowstone after bears began to raid traps. Eldon Saeugling is in foreground. He later became superintendent of the Guttenberg, Iowa federal fish hatchery. Saeugling collection.

INFORMATION SOURCES

Roger P. (Bill) Tanner was born April 18, near Saltillo, Mississippi. He entered into the service of the Bureau of Fisheries on May 3, 1923, and worked at the Upper Mississippi River Fish Rescue Division out of Homer, Minnesota and La Crosse, Wisconsin. This division was at large and subject to details anywhere east of the Rocky Mountains. He spent two seasons on rescue work and worked on details in Nebraska, Louisiana, Wisconsin, and Mississippi. He took a permanent detail at the trout hatchery at Windbar, Pennsylvania. In 1933, he was in charge of a new hatchery at Lamar, Pennsylvania. In 1953, he was transferred to Manchester, Iowa. He retired in 1965 after a total of 42 years and 5 days with the Federal Government. He provided a great deal of information that was used in the writing of this manuscript. I never knew him except through the mail, but he was a good friend of my father.

Bill Tanner at Buffalo Bill's hunting lodge, just east of Yellowstone Park. Tanner collection.

Hugh F. Tainter was born January 12, 1901, in Homer, Minnesota. His father, Frank L. Tainter, had entered the service of the Bureau of Fisheries in 1910 and helped in construction of the new Federal Fish Hatchery at Homer. Hugh began working as a seasonal employee for the Bureau starting in 1918, supplementing this temporary work with his personally-owned garage. He worked as a mechanic and on fish rescue crews. He worked in Yellowstone Park during the summers of 1927-29. In 1939, he married Rose Brommerich. When the hatchery at Homer closed in 1952, he was transferred to the hatchery at Guttenberg, Iowa, retiring in 1968. He died January 13, 1980. He had many happy memories of his Yellowstone experience and was proud of the work he had done there.

Hugh Tainter standing by 1-ton Reo Speedwagon fisheries truck, 1928. Tainter collection.

Eldon C. "Bud" Saeugling was born in Guttenberg, Iowa, November 30, 1906. He spent most of his career in government service as a fish culturist and biologist. His service in Yellowstone was from 1927 through 1932 during May, June, and July each year. He also spent one month (July) caring for the trout at the Mammoth fish rearing facility. He would then be detailed back to the Mississippi River for four months of fish rescue work. During his early career, in order to gain work experience, he requested details at 42 of the then 92 hatcheries in the United States during a 13-year period. In 1936, he married Mildred Winnall. His final work detail began in 1939 and was superintendent at the Guttenberg, Iowa, Federal Fish Hatchery. He retired in 1968 and died March 9, 1987.

Eldon Saeugling, June 1, 1928. Standing on cab of truck on way to Lake Hatchery. Snow is 15 feet deep. Saeugling collection.

Fay Copper was born August 30, 1904. He worked on the Ferryville, Wisconsin, seasonal fish rescue crews in the summers of 1921-23 and started as a regular employee at the Manchester, Iowa, hatchery in 1924. He spent 14 years working on the various fish cars and as captain of Fish Car No. 10 from 1937 to 1940. He subsequently worked 11 years at the Fairport, Iowa, hatchery and then transferred to Valley City, North Dakota, in 1951 as manager. In 1959, he transferred to the Rochester, Indiana, station. He retired in 1964 after 41 years of service with the Bureau of Fisheries and the Fish and Wildlife Service. He and his wife resided in Prairie du Chien, Wisconsin until his death.

Dewitt Clinton Booth, or D. C. as he preferred to be called because he disliked his first two names, was the youngest fish hatchery superintendent in the United States when he came to Spearfish, S. D., in 1899. He would occupy that post for the next 34 years.

He was born August 5, 1868 at Palatine Bridge, N. Y., grew up in New York and graduated from Colgate University. He began his career with the U.S. Customs Service and was assigned to work at the Columbian Exposition in Chicago in 1893. He soon transferred to the U. S. Bureau of Fisheries and worked at Cape Vincent, N. Y., Woods Hole, Mass., and Leadville, Colorado before transferring to the Spearfish fish hatchery. In 1901, he married Ruby Hines of Detroit, Michigan; and they had two children, Edward and Katherine.

During his time at Spearfish, many fish culturists were apprenticed to him; and these men later formed the core of the U. S. Bureau of Fisheries throughout the United States. Booth also developed many innovations and improvement in fish culture which were widely copied.

Booth died in 1938 while visiting his son in Texas.

Clarence F. Culler and Harry Canfield, superintendent of the La Crosse, Wisconsin, hatchery, both married sisters (Saeugling). Glen Leach, Chief of Fisheries in Washington, D. C., also married one of the sisters, all were from West Virginia. This made for a good family and business relationship. When at Homer, Mr. Culler instituted the Sea Scouts for La Crosse and Winona, some 200 boys in all. With his excellent contacts, he acquired by donation two large-sized sailing boats with a capacity of 100 boys each. These were used for sailing between La Crosse and Winona. This is when he was named Capt., of "Cap" Culler, a name he retained throughout his life. The Sea Scouts were eventually absorbed into the Boy Scouts program. He also earned the nickname "Paper Fish" because of voluminous reports he filed about the number of fish saved during the fish rescue operations. He was gifted for the position he held, keeping the 92 hatcheries operating to capacity, with many species produced for stocking waters throughout the United States and keeping everybody happy. He knew what people, from Congressmen to laymen, to contact for various favors in exchange for a carload of fish. He was a good ambassador. Capt. Culler died on January 16, 1953.

Captain Culler, with his secretaries Connie Hoffman and Hope Hosfraser, in front of the cruiser Avocet, late 1930's. Saeugling collection.

Remembrances of Hugh F. Tainter are based on stories he told F. H. Tainter as a young boy. This author has many more than those mentioned here. Recollections of Eldon Saeugling were based on a letter from him to F. H. Tainter in 1986. Those of Fay A. Copper were from a letter to F. H. Tainter in 1987. Recollections of Bill Tanner were from several letters to F. Tainter in 1986 and 1987.

Mrs. Harvey (Grace) Gordon was the daughter of E. E. Rote, an engineer at the Homer station from 1910-1929. She grew up at the station and was influenced by the scientists working there to study to become a teacher of biology. Her experiences while growing up there gave her considerable pleasure all her life. In 1973 she gave a presentation at the Winona County Historical Society meeting about the history of the fisheries station. Her notes were shared with Eunice Rhis, a childhood friend. Mrs. Rhis gave this author access to Mrs. Gordon's notes, some of which are included in this book.

All photographs provided by these cooperators were donated to the D. C. Booth National Fish Hatchery Museum and may be found in their archives.

Frank H. Tainter Ph.D.

An invaluable contributor to this endeavor was Arden Trandahl, former curator of the D. C. Booth National Fish Hatchery Museum. He provided many documents and photographs to the authors in preparation of this manuscript.

(Left) A young Bill Tanner and big catch from Atchataflaya Swamp, LA. (Right) Bill Tanner and Jimmy Depuis, near Soda Butte Hatchery, 1925. Both from Tanner collection.

The Booth's cottage at West Thumb, constructed in 1908.
D. C. Booth Historic Fish Hatchery Archives.

Ruby Booth washing clothes in hot spring, West Thumb.
D. C. Booth Historic Fish Hatchery Archives.

Frank H. Tainter Ph.D.

The Booth family, standing behind the bow of a Yellowstone Park Transportation Company excursion boat, probably at Lake Hotel boat dock, ca. 1908 or 1909. D. C. Booth Historic Fish Hatchery Archives.

Edward and Katherine Booth on Lake fish hatchery boat dock, ca. 1908 or 1909. D. C. Booth Historic Fish Hatchery Archives.

(Upper right) Fish car, chef Midler and Eugene Catte.
(Upper left) Fish Car No. 8, 1923.
(Middle left) Loading fish at Langdon, Kansas. Left to right
– Harold Catte, Bill Tanner, ?,?, Eugene Catte.
(Lower left) Eugene Catte Hatchery – Langdon, Kansas. Left to right – Bill Tanner, Eugene Catte, ?, Kate Catte, Harold Catte, men in pond unknown. 1924 or 1926.
All photos from Tanner collection.

Frank H. Tainter Ph.D.

NOTES FOR THE CHAPTERS

Acknowledgements

1. Varley, J. D. 1979. Record of egg shipments from Yellowstone fishes, 1914-1955. Yellowstone Inf. Paper No. 36, USFWA Yellowstone Aquatic Library, Yellowstone N. P., 45 pp.

The Setting

1. Haines, A. L. 1977. The Yellowstone Story – A History of Our First National Park. Vol. 2. Yellowstone Library and Museum Association, pp. 543, p. 88, quotation from a newspaper article published in 1868.

2. *Ibid.*, p. 5.

3. *Ibid.*, p. 88, quotation from a book by C. W. Cook *et al.*

4. *Ibid.*, p. 89.

5. *Ibid.*, p. 89.

6. *Ibid.*, p. 90, quotation from a reconnaissance of the park by D. S. Jordan in 1890.

The Fishes of Yellowstone

1. Varley, J. D. and P. Schullery. 1983. Freshwater Wilderness – Yellowstone Fishes and Their World. The Yellowstone Library and Museum Assoc., Yellowstone National Park, pp. 133. Information in this chapter was taken exclusively from this source. The distribution maps summarize much of that information.

2. Albright, Horace M., as told to Robert Cahn. 1985. The Birth of the National Park Service. Howe Brothers, Salt Lake City, Chicago. pp. 340. A portion of this photograph is shown on p. 191, and Albright relates an anecdote of this visit by the Crown Prince.

Spawn Collection and Fish Culture

1. Arnold, B. B. 1967. A ninety-seven-year history of fishery activities in Yellowstone National Park, Wyoming. Division of Fishery Services, BSFW. USFWS Yellowstone Aquatic Library, Yellowstone N. P., pp. 52.

2. D. C. Booth to A. E. Fuller, July 1, 1909. D. C. Booth Historic Fish Hatchery Archives.

3. D. C. Booth to Paul Washabaugh and Donald Smith, May 5, 1910. D. C. Booth Historic Fish Hatchery Archives.

4. D. C. Booth to Commissioner of Fisheries, February 25, 1909. D. C. Booth Historic Fish Hatchery Archives.

5. D. C. Booth to Paul Washabaugh and Donald Smith, May 5, 1910. D. C. Booth Historic Fish Hatchery Archives.

6. D. C. Booth to Charles Oliver Reed, April 27, 1909. D. C. Booth Historic Fish Hatchery Archives.

7. D. C. Booth to Commissioner of Fisheries, April 26, 1909. D. C. Booth Historic Fish Hatchery Archives.

8. D. C. Booth to Paul Washabaugh and Donald Smith, May 5, 1910. D. C. Booth Historic Fish Hatchery Archives.

9. Yellowstone Park log for 1909, Report by S. M. Ainsworth. D. C. Booth Historic Fish Hatchery Archives.

10. D. C. Booth to J. P. Snyder, June 8, 1904. D. C. Booth Fish Hatchery Museum Archives.

ARTIFICIAL SPAWNING

1. Smith, H. M. and W. C. Kendall. 1921. Fishes of the Yellowstone National Park. Bur. of Fisheries Doc. N. 904, pp. 30.

2. A series of photographs of the early fish collection operations on file in the Yellowstone Park Museum are dated as 1901-1920. This 1901 date probably is in error as Booth made special arrangements to photograph the fish cultural work and methods in 1909.

3. D. C. Booth to Glen C. Leach, April 28, 1909. D. C. Booth Historic Fish Hatchery Archives. Glen C. Leach volunteered the use of his camera. Very likely all the photographs in the series dated as 1901-1909 were taken in 1909. This seems to have been a very active year in the Yellowstone operation. It was also the year when the first fisheries motor launch was brought in.

ADMINISTRATION

1. D. C. Booth to Superintendent Thompson, July 8, 1912. D. C. Booth Historic Fish Hatchery Archives. This is a summary letter that Booth wrote shortly after his bout of depression and return following his resignation as superintendent of the Spearfish fish hatchery.

2. *Ibid.*

3. Arnold, B. B. A ninety-seven-year history of fishery activities in Yellowstone National Park, Wyoming. Division of Fishery Services, BSFW. USFWS Yellowstone Aquatic Library, Yellowstone N. P., pp. 52.

4. D. C. Booth to Superintendent Thompson, July 8, 1912. D. C. Booth Historic Fish Hatchery Archives.

5. Arnold, B. B. 1967. A ninety-seven-year history of fishery activities in Yellowstone National Park, Wyoming. Division of Fishery Services, BSFW. USFWS Yellowstone Aquatic Library, Yellowstone N. P., pp. 52.

6. D. C. Booth to Superintendent Thompson, July 8, 1912. D. C. Booth Historic Fish Hatchery Archives.

7. Arnold, B. B. 1967. A ninety-seven-year history of fishery activities in Yellowstone National Park, Wyoming. Division of Fishery Services, BSFW. USFWS Yellowstone Aquatic Library, Yellowstone N. P., pp. 52.

8. *Ibid.*

9. D. C. Booth to Commissioner of Fisheries, April 26, 1909. D. C. Booth Historic Fish Hatchery Archives.

10. D. C. Booth to Commissioner of Fisheries, May 5, 1909. D. C. Booth Historic Fish Hatchery Archives.

11. D. C. Booth to Commissioner of Fisheries, April 6, 1910. D. C. Booth Historic Fish Hatchery Archives.

12. D. C. Booth to R. O. Schleicher, March 6, 1911. D. C. Booth Historic Fish Hatchery Archives.

13. D. C. Booth to Commissioner of Fisheries, April 20, 1910. D. C. Booth Historic Fish Hatchery Archives.

14. D. C. Booth to Commissioner of Fisheries, March 15, 1911. D. C. Booth Historic Fish Hatchery Archives.

15. D. C. Booth to Commissioner of Fisheries, March 4, 1909. D. C. Booth Historic Fish Hatchery Archives.

16. Spearfish Station log, May, 1905. D. C. Booth Historic Fish Hatchery Archives.

17. Yellowstone Park log for 1909, Report by S. M. Ainsworth. D. C. Booth Historic Fish Hatchery Archives.

18. D. C. Booth to American Net and Twine Company, April 25, 1910. D. C. Booth Historic Fish Hatchery Archives.

19. Yellowstone Park log for 1909, Report by S. M. Ainsworth. D. C. Booth Historic Fish Hatchery Archives.

20. Log of Yellowstone Park West Side Station, 1910. D. C. Booth Historic Fish Hatchery Archives.

21. East-Side Yellowstone Park log, 1910. D. C. Booth Historic Fish Hatchery Archives.

22. Log of Lake Hotel Camp, 1910. D. C. Booth Historic Fish Hatchery Archives.

23. Alvord, William. 1975. History of fisheries management in Montana (1900-1975), USFWS Yellowstone Aquatic Library, Yellowstone N. P., pp. 97.

24. *Ibid.*

25. *Ibid.*

26. Thompson, W. T. 1914. Annual Report of the U. S. Fisheries Station, Bozeman, Montana. USFWS Yellowstone Aquatic Library, Yellowstone N. P.

27. Arnold, B. B. 1967. A ninety-seven-year history of fishery activities in Yellowstone National Park, Wyoming. Division of Fishery Services, BSFW. USFWS Yellowstone Aquatic Library, Yellowstone N. P., pp. 52.

28. *Ibid.*

29. Thompson, W. T. 1914. Annual Report of the U. S. Fisheries Station, Bozeman, Montana. USFWS Yellowstone Aquatic Library, Yellowstone N. P.

30. *Ibid.*

31. Thompson, W. T. 1915. Annual Report of the U. S. Fisheries Station, Bozemen, Montana. USFWS Yellowstone Aquatic Library, Yellowstone N. P.

32. Haines, A. L. 1977. The Yellowstone Story – A History of Our First National Park. Vol. 2. Yellowstone Library and Museum Assoc., pp. 543.

33. Thompson, W. T. 1917. Annual Report of the U. S. Fisheries Station, Bozeman, Montana. USFWS Yellowstone Aquatic Library, Yellowstone N. P.

34. The Winona Republican Herald, July 25, 1909, on file at the Winona County Historical Society, Winona, Minnesota.

35. The Winona Republican Herald, June 11, 1925, on file at the Winona County Historical Society, Winona, Minnesota.

36. Carlander, H. B. 1954. A history of fish and fishing in the upper Mississippi River. Upper. Miss. River Cons. Comm., pp. 96.

37. *Ibid.*

38. *Ibid.*

39. Anonymous. 1979. The fish car era. Dept. of Interior, U. S. Fish and Wildlife Service. Unnumbered pamphlet, pp. 16.

Development of the Facilities

1. Sheldon, F. 1936. History of the fish planting in Yellowstone National Park, USFWS Yellowstone Aquatic Library, Yellowstone N. P., pp. 16.

2. Arnold, B. B. 1967. A ninety-seven-year history of fishery activities in Yellowstone National Park, Wyoming. Division of Fishery Services, BSFW.

USFWS Yellowstone Aquatic Library, Yellowstone N. P., pp. 52.

3. Alvord, William. 1975. History of fisheries management in Montana (1900-1975), USFWS Yellowstone Aquatic Library, Yellowstone N. P., pp. 97.

4. Thompson, W. T. 1914. Annual Report of the U. S. Fisheries Station, Bozeman, Montana. USFWS Yellowstone Aquatic Library, Yellowstone N. P.

5. U. S. Bureau of Fisheries. 1916. Department of Commerce, Fisheries Service Bulletin No. 16.

6. U. S. Bureau of Fisheries. 1917. Department of Commerce, Fisheries Service Bulletin No. 27.

7. U. S. Bureau of Fisheries. 1917. Department of Commerce, Fisheries Bulletin No. 29.

8. *Ibid.*

9. U. S. Bureau of Fisheries. 1917. Department of Commerce, Fisheries Service Bulletin No. 28.

10. U. S. Bureau of Fisheries. 1917. Department of Commerce, Fisheries Service Bulletin No. 29.

11. U. S. Bureau of Fisheries. 1921. Department of Commerce, Fisheries Service Bulletin No. 76.

12. U. S. Bureau of Fisheries. 1924. Department of Commerce, Fisheries Service Bulletin No. 112.

13. Albright, Horace M. 1929. Report on the construction of the Lake and Mammoth Fish Hatchery, Season of 1929. Nat. Park Service, pp. 14.

14. Albright, Horace M., as told to Robert Cahn. 1985. The Birth of the National Park Service. Howe Brothers, Salt Lake City, Chicago. pp. 340.

15. Albright, Horace M. 1929. Report on the construction of the Lake and Mammoth Fish Hatchery, Season of 1929. Nat. Park Service, pp. 14.

16. Albright, Horace M., as told to Robert Cahn. 1985. The Birth of the National Park Service. Howe Brothers, Salt Lake City, Chicago. pp. 340.

17. Albright, Horace M. 1929. Report on the construction of the Lake and Mammoth Fish Hatchery, Season of 1929. Nat. Park Service, pp. 14.

18. Anonymous. Undated. Final construction report on account 777, donation in the amount of $15,000 for construction in connection with furthering fish propagation at Lake Yellowstone in Yellowstone National Park. Appropriation 4 x 470 National Park Service donations. File No. 164-X222. USFWS Yellowstone Aquatic Library, Yellowstone N. P., pp. 4. plus figures.

19. Arnold, B. B. 1967. A ninety-seven-year history of fishery activities in Yellowstone National Park, Wyoming. Division of Fishery Services, BSFW. USFWS Yellowstone Aquatic Library, Yellowstone N. P. pp. 52.

20. Albright, Horace M. 1929. Report on the construction of the Lake and Mammoth Fish Hatchery, Season of 1929. Nat. Park Service, pp. 14.

21. *Ibid.*

22. Arnold, B. B. 1967. A ninety-seven-year history of fishery activities in Yellowstone Park, Wyoming. Division of Fishery Services, BSFW. USFWS Yellowstone Aquatic Library, Yellowstone N. P. pp. 52.

Fish Lake

1. Smith, H. M. and W. C. Kendall. 1921. Fishes of the Yellowstone National Park. Bur. of Fisheries Doc. N. 804, pp. 30.

2. Mitchell, S. W. 1880. Through the Yellowstone Park to Fort Custer. Lippincott's Magazine 26 (July):21-41.

3. Varley, J. D. and P. Schullery. 1983. Freshwater Wilderness – Yellowstone Fishes and Their World. The Yellowstone Library and Museum Assoc., Yellowstone National Park, pp. 133.

4. *Ibid.*

5. Haines, A. L. 1977. The Yellowstone Story – A History of Our First National Park. Vol. 2. Yellowstone Library and Museum Association, pp. 543.

6. *Ibid.*

7. Arnold, B. B. 1967. A ninety-seven-year history of fishery activities in Yellowstone National Park, Wyoming. Division of Fishery Services, BSFW. USFWS Yellowstone Aquatic Library, Yellowstone N. P. pp. 52.

8. *Ibid.*

9. *Ibid.*

10. U. S. Bureau of Fisheries. 1922. Department of Commerce, Fisheries Service Bulletin No. 86.

11. U. S. Bureau of Fisheries. 1923. Department of Commerce, Fisheries Service Bulletin No. 98.

12. U. S. Bureau of Fisheries. 1927. Department of Commerce, Fisheries Service Bulletin No. 146.

13. U. S. Bureau of Fisheries. 1923. Department of Commerce, Fisheries Service Bulletin No. 98.

14. U. S. Bureau of Fisheries. 1922. Department of Commerce, Fisheries Service Bulletin No. 86.

15. Arnold, B. B. 1967. A ninety-seven-year history of fishery activities in Yellowstone National Park, Wyoming. Division of Fishery Services, BSFW. USFWS Yellowstone Aquatic Library, Yellowstone N. P. pp. 52.

16. *Ibid.*

17. *Ibid.*

18. Varley, J. D. 1979. Record of egg shipments from Yellowstone fishes, 1914-1955. Yellowstone Inf. Paper No. 36, pp. 45.

19. Arnold, B. B. 1967. A ninety-seven-year history of fishery activities in Yellowstone National Park, Wyoming. Division of Fishery Services, BSFW. USFWS Yellowstone Aquatic Library, Yellowstone N. P. pp. 52.

20. Varley, J. D. 1979. Record of egg shipments from Yellowstone fishes, 1914-1955. Yellowstone Inf. Paper No. 36, pp. 45.

The Boats

1. Arnold, B. B. 1967. A ninety-seven-year history of fishery activities in Yellowstone National Park, Wyoming. Division of Fishery Services, BSFW. USFWS Yellowstone Aquatic Library, Yellowstone N. P. pp. 52.

2. D. C. Booth to Camden Anchor-Rockland Machine Company, February 8, 1909. D. C. Booth Historic Fish Hatchery Archives.

3. D. C. Booth to Commissioner of Fisheries, February 15, 1909. D. C. Booth Historic Fish Hatchery Archives.

4. D. C. Booth to Stanley and Patterson, May 30, 1910. D. C. Booth Historic Fish Hatchery Archives.

5. D. C. Booth to Commissioner of Fisheries, February 15, 1909. D. C. Booth Historic Fish Hatchery Archives.

6. Carlander, H. B. 1954. A history of fish and fishing in the upper Mississippi River. Upper Miss. River Cons. Comm., pp. 96.

The Way There

1. Haines, A. L. 1977. The Yellowstone Story – A History of Our First National Park. Vol. 2. Yellowstone Library and Museum Association, pp. 543.

2. *Ibid.*

3. *Ibid.*

4. U. S. Bureau of Fisheries. 1927. Department of Commerce, Fisheries Service Bulletin No. 146.

5. Thompson, W. T. 1918. Annual Report of the U. S. Fisheries Station, Bozeman, Montana, USFWS Yellowstone Aquatic Library, Yellowstone N. P.

6. U. S. Bureau of Fisheries. 1927. Department of Commerce, Fisheries Service Bulletin No. 146.

7. *Ibid.*

Bear Me in Mind

1. Thompson, W. T. 1915. Annual Report of the U. S. Fisheries Station, Bozeman, Montana, USFWS Yellowstone Aquatic Library, Yellowstone N. P.

2. U. S. Bureau of Fisheries. 1916. Department of Commerce, Fisheries Service Bulletin No. 16.

3. U. S. Bureau of Fisheries. 1917. Department of Commerce, Fisheries Service Bulletin No. 28.

4. Thompson, W. T. 1915. Annual Report of the U. S. Fisheries Station, Bozeman, Montana, WSFWS Yellowstone Aquatic Library, Yellowstone N. P.

THE BOAT DRAWINGS

The following three pages contain drawings and measurements of U. S. Fisheries Boat No. 39. This is the boat presently on the grounds of the D. C. Booth Federal Fish Hatchery Museum.

Boat No. 39, as discovered in Corwin Springs, Montana in 1989, before restoration. Tainter collection.

Fish Culture in Yellowstone National Park

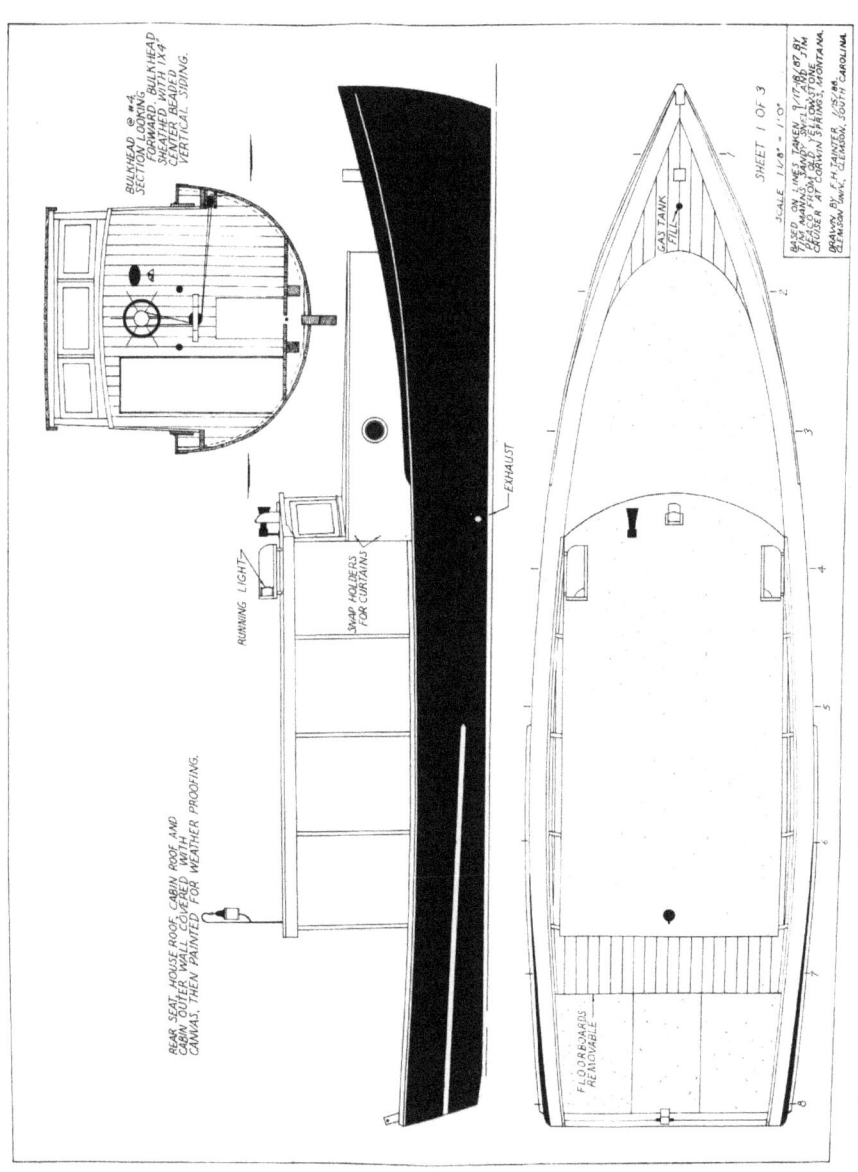

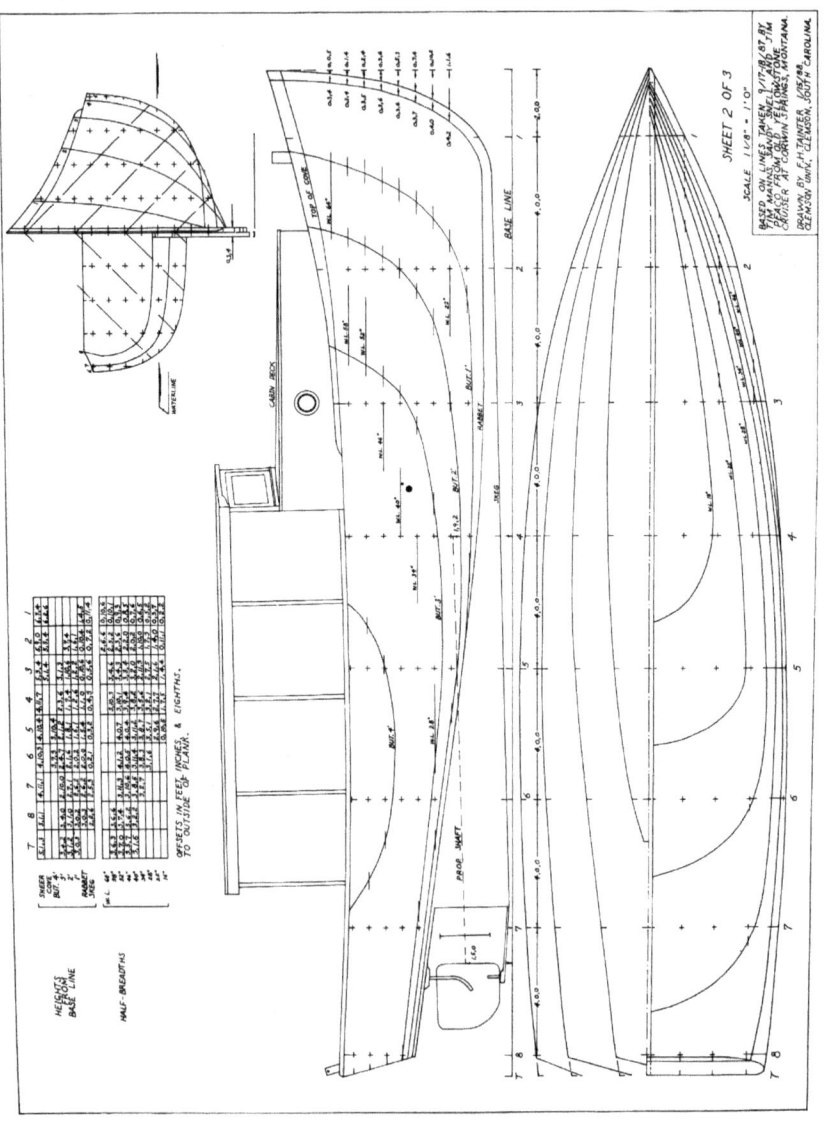

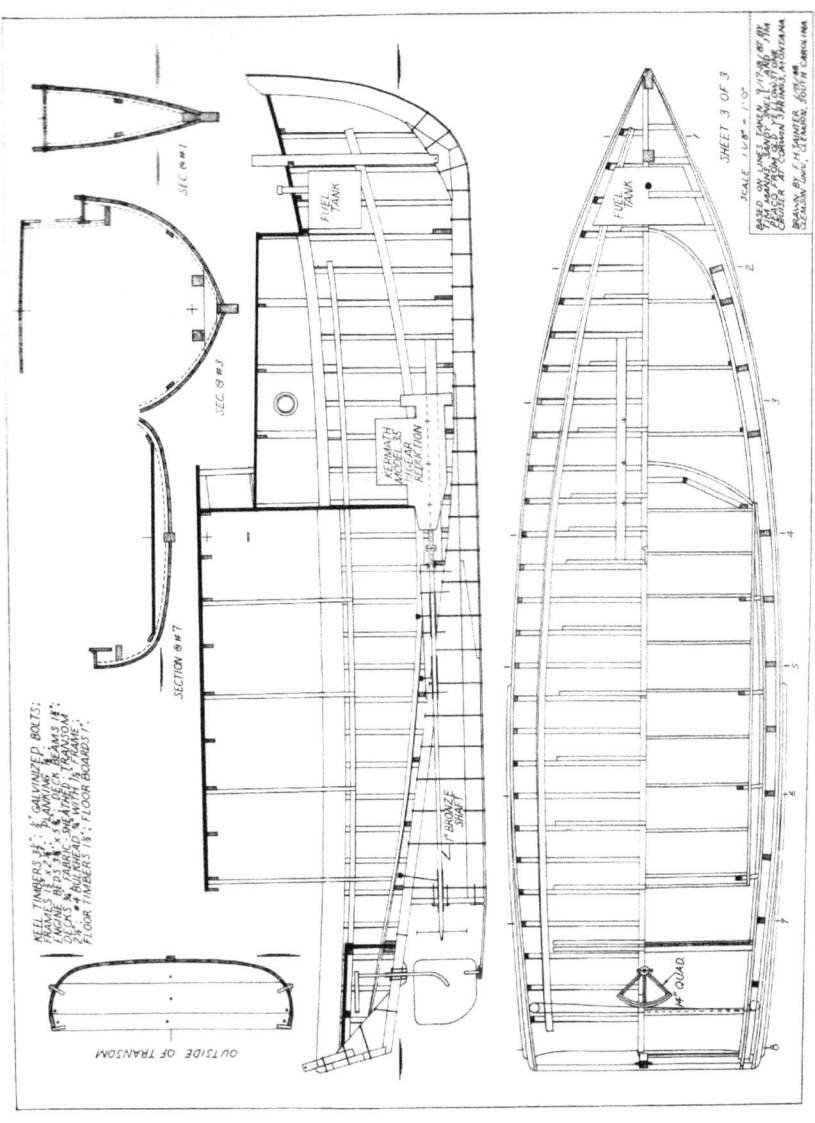

ADDITIONAL PHOTOS

(Left) Bill Tanner and fish trap at Clear Creek. (Right) Bill Tanner at the Soda Butte Hatchery. Tanner collection.

Jim Bonner, Bill Tanner, W. C. Bunch collecting eggs, Peale Island. Tanner collection.

(Left) Clyde Adams, Bill Tanner, Swamp Walker, Mr. Lillybridge, and old Ruff. (Right) Cabin at Clear Creek. Tanner collection.

Cabin at Clear Creek, built by Clyde Adams, Swamp Walker, and Bill Tanner. Tanner collection.

The Homer, Minnesota, Federal Fish Hatchery, showing the newly constructed boat house (largest building), the laboratory, some ponds, and two workers' houses (foreground). Saeugling collection.

Fish rescue work in a land-locked slough of the Mississippi River. Saeugling collection.

Fish Culture in Yellowstone National Park

*Fish rescue work in a land-locked slough near Wyalusing, Iowa.
Saeugling collection.*

*Fish rescue work near Clayton, Iowa.
Saeugling collection.*

More fish rescue work. Note bluffs in background.
Saeugling collection.

Releasing rescued fish back into the Mississippi River.
Saeugling collection.

*On the Yellowstone Trail, near Bismark, North Dakota.
Saeugling collection.*

*The new bunkhouse at Lake.
Saeugling collection.*

(Upper left) The road into Lake, Ray Sampson in center. (Upper right) Eldon Saeugling at Grouse Creek, 1929. (Lower) Fish trap at Pelican Creek, 1930. Saeugling collection.

(Right) The new cabin at Peale Island, 1929. (Lower) Bill Tanner (left) and Eldon Saeugling cutting firewood at Peale Island. Saeugling collection.

The fisheries Reo Speed Wagon truck at Mt. Washburn. Saeugling collection.

The boat dock at Lake. Note the cowboy garb worn by most of the individuals. Saeugling collection.

Two of the 35' cabin cruisers at Lake. Saeugling collection.

Eldon Saeugling and "Bubbles" at Lake, 1931. Saeugling collection.

RECIPE FROM FISH CAR NO. 10–SPANISH OMELET

Courtesy of Nancy Hook, daughter of Roger Tanner.
1 ½ tablespoon lard
1 green pepper chopped fine
1 small stalk celery chopped fine 6 onions chopped fine
? red pepper to taste
black pepper and salt to taste

Stew until brown about 40 minutes in frying pan. Add 1 No. 2 can of tomato puree and let stew for 20 min. Then add 2 tablespoons of peas, let stew for 15 min.

Use with egg omelet anyway desired.